KARL SHAPIRO

GARLAND REFERENCE LIBRARY
OF THE HUMANITIES
(VOL. 131)

Kay Kyser reading in New Guinea in 1943.

KARL SHAPIRO
A Descriptive Bibliography 1933–1977

Lee Bartlett

with a foreword by
James Woodress
and a checklist of criticism and reviews by
David Huwiler

GARLAND PUBLISHING, INC. • NEW YORK & LONDON
1979

James Woodress's foreword, with the exception of the first
paragraph, is reprinted with the permission of The
Macmillan Press, Ltd., London, from *Contemporary Writers
of the English Language*.

Library of Congress Cataloging in Publication Data

Bartlett, Lee, 1950–
    Karl Shapiro.

    (Garland reference library of the humanities ; v. 131)
    Includes index.
    1. Shapiro, Karl Jay, 1913–   —Bibliography.
Z8813.25.B37 [PS3537.H27]   016.811'5'2   78-68245
ISBN 0-8240-9812-9

Printed on acid-free, 250-year-life paper
Manufactured in the United States of America

for Lebaron Albert Bartlett
&
Mary, who wrote,
"And the dream birds circle,
Singing our lives."

CONTENTS

ILLUSTRATIONS

FOREWORD

It is an unusual privilege to be able to write an introduction to a book by a friend that deals with the work of another friend. Lee Bartlett, my tennis partner and student, has compiled a long-needed bibliography of the writings of Karl Shapiro, who has been my friend and colleague for a decade in the English Department of the University of California at Davis. This work supersedes the earlier bibliography put together by William White at Wayne State University in 1960 and supplemented by Layton Damiano's unpublished checklist compiled at Davis in 1975. It is complete and up to date through 1977. It no doubt will have to be revised and expanded sometime in the future, because Shapiro shows no signs of putting his typewriter in mothballs or pensioning off his muse. For the time being, however, it fills a real need, and I am pleased to have a modest part in the enterprise.

Karl Shapiro is a poet of great versatility with a sophisticated command of prosody and a sharp ear for speech rhythms and verbal harmonies. He also is a man of considerable erudition, though he never finished college, and a serious though good-humored social critic. Since his first volume of poems was printed privately in 1935, he has published continuously during the subsequent four-plus decades. As poet and critic, he always has taken an iconoclastic stance. He attacks intellectual poetry, poseurs, stuffed shirts, and the establishment with great vigor and as a result has been a controversial figure. As editor of *Poetry* and *The Prairie Schooner* for sixteen years, he was a significant force in contemporary poetry, and as a professor he has taught two decades of aspiring writers.

When Shapiro published *Selected Poems* (1968), he ignored his first volume, about which he writes in "Recapitulations":

My first small book was nourished in the dark,
Secretly written, published, and inscribed.

> Bound in wine-red, it made no brilliant mark.
> Rather impossible relatives subscribed.

His first recognition came in 1941 when he appeared in *Five Young American Poets*, published by New Directions. During the next four years, while he was in the army in the Southwest Pacific, he brought out four volumes. Two of them are important: *Person, Place and Thing* and Pulitzer Prize-winning *V-Letter and Other Poems*. The former contains excellent poems of social comment in traditional form. "The Dome of Sunday" comments in sharp, clear imagery cast in blank verse on urban "Row houses and row-lives"; "Drug Store" observes youth culture satirically in unrhymed stanzas; "University [of Virginia]" mounts a low-keyed attack: "To hurt the Negro and avoid the Jew / Is the curriculum."

V-Letter and Other Poems contains some of the best poems to come out of World War II, some of which are "V-Letter," "Elegy for a Dead Soldier," "Troop Train," "The Gun," "Sunday: New Guinea," and "Christmas Eve: Australia." The form usually is rhymed stanzas, even *terza rima*, and here Shapiro's social comment finds a wider context. There also begin to be foreshadowings of later preoccupations: religious themes and attacks on intellectualism. "The Jew" anticipates *Poems of a Jew*, and "The Intellectual" ("I'd rather be a barber and cut hair / Than to walk with you in gilt museum halls") looks toward attacks on Pound and Eliot in *The Defense of Ignorance*.

Although Shapiro does not write long poems (the exception being *Essay on Rime*, a youthful treatise on the art of poetry in which "Everything was going to be straightened out"), *Poems, 1940–1953* contains an evocative seven-part sequence telling the story of Adam and Eve. (This interest in myth reasserts itself in *Adult Bookstore* in a poignant version in 260 lines of "The Rape of Philomel.") This volume also contains "Israel," occasioned by the founding of that country, and it must have inspired *Poems of a Jew*.

> When I see the name of Israel high in print
> The fences crumble in my flesh . . .

Shapiro grew up in a Russian-Jewish family not particularly religious, and after his bar mitzvah, "I lost all interest in what I had learned." But *Poems of a Jew* explores his Jewishness with pride, wit, and irony, beginning with "Alphabet" ("letters . . . strict as flames," "black and clean" and bristling "like barbed wire").

As early as 1942 Shapiro had published a prose-poem, "The Dirty Word," but in 1964 he turned to this form exclusively in *The Bourgeois Poet*, dropping the kind of verses he previously had thought best, "the poem with a beginning, a middle, and an end . . . that used literary allusion and rhythmic structuring and intellectual argument." He wanted a medium in which he could say anything he pleased—ridiculous, nonsensical, obscene, autobiographical, pompous. The individual pieces cover a wide variety of topics and, as earlier, they comment on persons, places, things. The longest (fourteen pages), "I am an atheist who says his prayers," which reminds one of Shapiro's enthusiasm for Whitman, could have been called "Song of Myself." These prose-poems (or free verse set as prose paragraphs) had a mixed reception. But Adrienne Rich noted that in his new style Shapiro was going through a "constant revising and purifying of his speech," as all poets must, and she thought parts of the volume were a "stunning success."

In *White-Haired Lover*, a cycle of middle-aged love poems, Shapiro returned to traditional forms, often the sonnet. This also is true of *Adult Bookstore*, a collection that ranges widely in subject. "The Humanities Building," "A Parliament of Poets," and the title poem show that Shapiro has not lost the wit, irony, and technique that always have characterized his work. "The Heiligenstadt Testament" is a splendid dramatic monologue of Beethoven's deathbed delirium, and among the poems occasioned by his move to California are "Garage Sale" ("This situation . . . / Strikes one as a cultural masterpiece") and a perfect Petrarchan sonnet on freeways and California suburbia.

The Poetry Wreck, which contains Shapiro's most important critical statements, throws light on his poetry, his sources, his beliefs. The derogatory essays on Pound and Eliot are reprinted along with admiring appraisals of W.H. Auden ("Eliot and Pound had rid the poem of emotion completely. . . . Auden reversed the process"), William Carlos Williams ("whose entire literary career has been dedicated to the struggle to preserve spontaneity and immediacy of experience"), Whitman, Dylan Thomas, Henry Miller, and Randall Jarrell. Jarrell, whose "poetry I admired and looked up to most after William Carlos Williams," once said in a passage Shapiro quotes: "Karl Shapiro's poems are fresh and young and rash and live; their hard clear outline, their flat bold colors create a world like that of a knowing and skillful neo-primitive painting, without any of the confusion or profundity of atmosphere, or aerial perspective, but with notable visual and satiric force."

James Woodress

INTRODUCTION

William White's *Karl Shapiro: A Bibliography* appeared in 1960 in connection with Wayne State University's exhibition of the poet's manuscripts and books from the Charles Feinberg Collection. Although it was accurate and complete, eighteen years have passed since its publication. Karl Shapiro is a major American poet and essayist of the second half of this century; clearly a descriptive and current bibliography is overdue.

The present volume attempts to record all books, pamphlets, and broadsides written, coauthored, edited, and introduced by Karl Shapiro from 1933 to 1977. In addition, the poet's periodical appearances are noted, as well as Shapiro's contributions to anthologies and translations of his work. David Huwiler has appended a checklist of selected criticism and reviews of Shapiro's poetry.

Section A describes all first editions of the poet's books, pamphlets, and broadsides. A typical entry contains the following information:

Edition statement: The initial heading of each entry identifies title, date of publication, and edition.

Title page: A quasi-facsimile transcription of the title page.

Collation: Pagination shows the numbering or inferred numbering of each page; size of the item in inches; type of paper, whether laid or wove. As almost all of Shapiro's books have been produced by modern machine methods, I have not collated signatures.

Pagination: Contents of each page, often described in quasi-facsimile.

Binding: Color of cloth; quasi-facsimile transcription of all printing or stamping on covers and spine; description of endpapers.

Dust jacket: Color of paper and printing; quasi-facsimile transcription of printing on covers and spine, as well as flyleaves.

Publication: Available facts concerning publication, including publisher, date published, printer, and price.

Contents: List of poems and/or articles included, with page numbers.

Notes: In March 1978, the compiler interviewed Karl Shapiro at his home in Davis, California. During that time the poet commented on the publishing history of several of his books, with the warning that his memory might not be quite accurate. Those comments follow a number of entries; they are given in italics *without* quotation marks. In addition, quotations from a number of Shapiro's prefaces and introductions to his own books are included in italics *within* quotation marks.

Section B includes books and pamphlets coauthored, edited, or introduced by Shapiro; it is also descriptive as above. Section C includes the poet's contributions to periodicals; at the head of each entry distinction is made between poems and prose; all of the poet's major published articles, reviews, and letters are annotated, usually with selections from the pieces themselves. Section D draws together many of Shapiro's appearances in anthologies; here an attempt has been made to be representative rather than complete. Section E lists Shapiro's work which has been translated into foreign languages. The Appendix is a checklist of selected criticism and reviews of the poet's work compiled by David Huwiler. As with Section D, it is thorough but representative rather than exhaustive; major entries in part one (biography and criticism) are annotated.

It is not the province of this bibliography to cover nonprint media, though one major item should be mentioned. In 1976, Pyramid Films released "Karl Shapiro's America," a thirteen-minute color film written by the poet and directed and produced by Arthur Hoyle. According to the advertisement, the film is "an introduction to the poems and literary viewpoint of Karl Shapiro, in which photos, paintings, and collages visualize the verbal impressions of everyday America. Interspersed are comments by Shapiro on his work and its reflection of American middle class life."

By way of acknowledgment I would like to thank first Karl Shapiro, who gave me free run of his collection of first editions, magazines, and manuscripts; he cheerfully endured all manner of questions about his life and work, submitted to a formal interview, provided numerous names and addresses, and allowed me to quote extensively from his articles and reviews. I am of course indebted to William White for laying the bibliographic foundation in 1960, as well as Layton Damiano for compiling an unpublished checklist of much of Shapiro's work in 1975. A special thanks goes to the entire American literature group at the University of California, Davis—Everett Carter, Peter Hays, Jack Hicks, Brom Weber, Robert Wiggins, and especially David Robertson, who took the photographs of Shapiro's title pages which are included here, and Michael J. Hoffman, who gave me time from my dissertation to complete this project. It was James Woodress who first suggested the idea of this bibliography to me; I wish to thank him not only for his constant encouragement and counsel, but also for his never-flagging optimism both in the classroom and on the tennis court. Finally, I am especially grateful to my wife, Mary, who once again set aside her own work so that I might use the desk and typewriter for another of my interminable projects; she has borne with good humor piles of books, magazines, notecards, and paper for months, to say nothing of a distracted and preoccupied spouse.

Davis, California Lee Bartlett

CHRONOLOGY

1913	Born in Baltimore, Maryland, November 10
1932–33	Attended the University of Virginia
1935	First book, *Poems*, published
1937–39	Attended The Johns Hopkins University
1940	Attended Pratt Library School, Baltimore
1941	*Five Young American Poets*
1941–45	United States Army; service in the Medical Corps in the South Pacific and the OSS in Washington, D.C.
1942	Jeanette Sewell Davis Prize, *Poetry Magazine*; *Person, Place and Thing*; *The Place of Love*
1943	Levinson Prize, *Poetry Magazine*; Contemporary Poetry Prize
1944	*V-Letter and Other Poems*; grant from the American Academy of Arts and Letters
1945	Pulitzer Prize for Poetry; Shelley Memorial Prize; *Essay on Rime*; married Evelyn Katz
1945–46	Fellow in American Letters, Library of Congress; Guggenheim Fellow
1946–47	Consultant in Poetry, Library of Congress
1947	*Trial of a Poet and Other Poems*
1947–50	Associate Professor of English, The Johns Hopkins University
1948	*A Bibliography of Modern Prosody*

1950–56	Editor, *Poetry Magazine*
1952	Lecturer, Salzburg Seminar in American Studies
1953	*Poems 1940–1953*; Montgomery Lectureship in Contemporary Civilization, University of Nebraska; *Beyond Criticism*
1953–55	Editor, *The Newberry Library Bulletin*; Guggenheim Fellow
1955	Lecturer, India, United States State Department
1955–57	Visiting Professor of English, University of California, Berkeley and Davis, and University of Indiana, Bloomington
1956	Fellow, Kenyon School of Letters, Summer
1956–66	Professor of English, University of Nebraska
1956–66	Editor, *Prairie Schooner*
1957	Fellow, Kenyon School of Letters, Summer
1958	*Poems of a Jew*
1959	Elliston Lecturer, University of Cincinnati; member of the National Institute of Arts and Letters
1960	*American Poetry, In Defense of Ignorance, Start with the Sun*
1961	Eunice Tietjens Memorial Prize, *Poetry Magazine*
1962	*Prose Keys to Modern Poetry*
1963	Oscar Blumenthal Prize, *Poetry Magazine*
1964	*The Bourgeois Poet*
1965	*A Prosody Handbook*
1966–68	Professor of English, University of Illinois, Chicago Circle

1967   Divorced from Evelyn Katz; married Teri Kovach

1968   *The Soldier's Tale* performed at The University of
        Chicago; *Selected Poems, To Abolish Children and Other
        Essays, White-Haired Lover*

1968–   Professor of English, University of California,
        Davis

1969   Bollingen Prize for Poetry

1971–   Editorial Board, *The California Quarterly*

1971   *Edsel*

1975   *The Poetry Wreck*

1976   Film, *Karl Shapiro's America*; judge, Hart Crane
        Memorial Poetry Contest, *The California Quarterly*;
        Adult Bookstore

A. BOOKS, PAMPHLETS, BROADSIDES

A1   POEMS   1935

Poems / Karl Jay Shapiro / Baltimore, Maryland / 1935

Collation: pp. [1-4] 5-64; 7 3/8" x 5 1/8"; printed
on laid paper.

Pagination: p. [1] half-title, p. [2] statement of
limitation, p. [3] title page, p. [4] dedication,
copyright, pp. 5-6 Contents, pp. 7-64 text.

Binding: Dark red cloth over boards. Stamped in gold
on spine, reading downwards: POEMS BY KARL JAY SHAPIRO.
White endpapers.

Dust jacket: Issued without dust jacket.

Publication: Two hundred copies, signed & numbered,
privately printed by the Waverly Press, Inc., Baltimore,
Maryland, March 15, 1935.

Contents: 7 "The Forethought," 8 "Indemnity," 9 "Affir-
mation," 10 "Negation," 11 "And Music at the Close,"
12 "Admonition," 13 "Conceit on Parting," 14 "Desiring
This Man's Art," 15 "Memory," 16 "Genesis," 17 "Nati-
vity," 18 "Thoroughfare," 19 "Bouquet," 20 "Rondeau,"
21 "Triolet to His Mistress' Eyebrow," 22 "No Penance
Due to Innocence," 23 "Gladdith Anon, Thou Lusty
Troynovaunt," 24 "Ferdinand," 26 "Malvolio," 27 "Elec-
tra's Peasant," 28 "While Greasy Joan Doth Keel the
Pot," 29 "Hothouse Aisle," 30 "Lilies of the Valley,"
31 "More Sinned Against Than," 32 "Simile," 33 "Anaes-
thesia Etude," 34 "Public Transit," 35 "Apostrophe of
the Bitter Fool," 36 "Afterthought," 37 "Aphonos,"
38 "(Revenge)," 39 "Aorist," 40 "Joy Ride," 41 "Per-
petual Benediction," 42 "Shenandoah," 43 "There Are
Birds," 44 "Appetite," 45 "Appetite II," 46 "Suburban,"
47 "Tatterdemalion," 48 "And Fugue," 49 "Prostitute,"
50 "Esplanade," 51 "Movie," 52 "Jazz Hit," 53 "Morning
Sky," 54 "Soliloquy from an Ivory Tower," 55 "Ireni-
con," 64 "Doxology."

*Note: I don't remember how I decided to publish my
first book, but I know I wanted to publish one. An
uncle of mine who was a customhouse broker had a medical
publishing company for a customer in Baltimore,
Williams & Wilkens. They were an old established company who had never published any literature, but my
uncle introduced me to somebody there who told me they
would publish my book for a couple hundred dollars.
I didn't have any money; my uncle put that up, hoping
he'd get it back--he didn't. The books weren't distributed by the company; when they were ready I simply
picked them up and either sold them or gave them away
to friends and relatives. The bulk of them were eventually destroyed, I guess. When I was drafted, I left
them with a friend because she was going to try to sell
them. But she moved several times and the books just
evaporated.*

A2 THE PLACE OF LOVE   1942

(a) *First edition:*

[in green:] THE PLACE OF LOVE / KARL SHAPIRO

Collation: pp. [1-4] 5 [6] 7 [8] 9-31 [32] 33 [34] 35-
45 [46] 47 [48] 49-53 [54] 55-69 [70] 71-78 [79-80];
8 7/8" x 5 5/8"; printed on wove paper.

Pagination: p. [1] title page, p. [2] copyright, p. [3]
CONTENTS, p. [4] blank, p. 5 PREFACE, p. [6] blank, p.
7 section number & poem titles, p. [8] blank, pp. 9-31
text, p. [32] blank, p. 33 section number & poem titles,
p. [34] blank, pp. 35-45 text, p. [46] blank, p. 47
section number, poem title, & epigraph, p. [48] blank,
pp. 49-52 text, p. 53 section number & poem titles, p.
[54] blank, pp. 55-68 text, p. 69 section number & poem
titles, p. [70] blank, pp. 71-78 text, p. [79] blank,
p. [80] printer's address.

Binding: Pale green cloth over boards. Stamped in green
on spine, reading downwards: THE PLACE OF LOVE KARL
SHAPIRO.

Dust jacket: Issued in yellow dust jacket, printed in green on front: The Place of Love / Karl Shapiro Sgt. U. S. Army. Born Baltimore, Mary- / land, 1913. Widely publicized for work in *Five / Young American Poets,* New Directions Press and / prize winning poems *Poetry Magazine*, Chicago, 1940, / 1941, 1942. Most recent American book, *Person / Place and Thing*, Reynal and Hitchcock, New York. / The Place of Love. Lyrics, Incantational prose-poems, / excerpts from letters written in Australia. Whereas / before his work was sharply satirical of modern life, / this volume is a highly personal experiment. / Karl Shapiro. On jacket spine, reading downwards: THE PLACE OF LOVE KARL SHA-PIRO.

Publication: Published by Cecily Crozier, editor of *A Comment*, an Australian avant-garde magazine. Although there is no copyright date available, Karl Shapiro remembers this book published prior to A3, sometime during the late summer of 1942. Printing by the Bradley Printers, Malvern, Australia.

Contents: 5 Preface, 9 "The New Ring," 10 "The Jewels," 12 "Portrait of My Hand," 13 "At Death's Door," 15 "The Egyptian Silk," 16 "The Scar," 18 "Syllabus," 19 "Mutability," 20 "My Hair," 22 "Conversation with a Vulture," 24 "The Dirty Word," 25 "A Sibyl," 27 "Necrophilist," 28 "The Sacred Bed," 30 "Mirror Distortion," 31 "Melbourne," 35 "Ostrich Feather," 37 "The Place of Love," 39 "Plot for a Short Story," 40 "War Poem," 41 "The Vigil," 43 "There Are Three Things," 45 "The Aunt," 49 "Bath-Sheba," 56 "A Cut Flower," 57 "Piano," 59 "The Immaterial Joy," 62 "Metempsychosis," 64 "The Tongue," 66 "Hotel De Luxe," 67 "Pressed Flower," 68 "The Voyage," 71 "A Flower," 73 "Confessio Amantis."

Note: Karl Shapiro's copy of the book was bound by the publisher in Kangaroo hide, stamped in green on spine as above. The poet once began to revise A2a, and in his copy the following changes are noted in pencil:

p. 37, "For of all life, man only is ashamed to be seen to love and copulate." [deleted]

p. 38, "For the sex is troubled, morning noon and night, in infancy and on the death bed, and before and after satiety." [deleted]

p. 38, "Hardening the nipples. Whether the groin is kicked or the penis symbolically detached." [deleted]

p. 38, "For deep is the disparity of the means between the sexes, the male creating his ugliness with his clothes, and the female worshipping her dress and her nakedness from childhood." [deleted]

p. 38, "Neither is there any clue to the high or the low, but we stand between and learn in our own way. For cold and lewd are the closed lips of death, and warm and pure are the open lips of the newly born." [deleted]

p. 73, Sections one & two deleted entire.

p. 75, "Quare tristis es, anima mea, et quare conturbas me?" [deleted]

p. 76, Section four deleted entire.

p. 77, "I confess that the tongue can project but three inches beyond the head. Similarly with the mobile and the elevator limbs and members. Nevertheless I entered the neighboring body with levers and with manufactured fingers—this I confess." [deleted]

p. 78, "I confess that the effect is greater than the achievement." [deleted]

p. 78, "and bride of my carnality," [deleted; "confession" entered below "carnality"—also deleted]

p. [79], "O book of the bride and bride of the book" [entered in pencil]

The Preface to A2 reads as follows: "A Personal book is made for personal readers. In an age of wars, in war-time, and in the midst of war, such a volume

*is almost certain to be condemned, or what is just as
serious to the writer, ignored. We have been brought
up to shun the lyrical ego, to look at ourselves from
without, to make a science of our acts. The poet in
particular has reacted to a revolution in knowledge
by developing the most advanced self-consciousness
possible, an intolerance for his own personality that
is just short of madness.*

*"Perhaps we are no longer (or not yet) equipped
to present poems of this nature. Writing this book I
found myself with Lenin in one hand and the Old Testament in the other, although with little sense of desperation or loss of joy in the adventure. But looking
back, I suspect a hidden panic; namely, Was this to be
the last personal moment?*

*"Each modern soldier acts under a similar compul-
sion and panic; but the book which was intended to be
a last look back is perhaps only a first look around.
For a time I closed my eyes and ears to 'the war-love
pattern of every other,' becoming conscious of the
power and the monotony of the configuration only much
later. The Place of Love was written from the inside
out: the bias and the original impress are therefore
still chiefly personal.*

*"The isolated sentences and paragraphs are ex-
tracted from letters written during the progress of
the book. I have endeavored to bind the prose poems
to the lyrics by means of these clues, and through
them and the general arrangement to provide some sequence of narrative."*

(b) *First paper edition:*

*Title page, Collation, Pagination, Publication, & Con-
tents* as A2a, save measures 9" x 5 1/2".

Binding: Issued in stiff pale gray paper covers.
Printed in green on front cover: The Place of Love /
Karl Shapiro. Printed in green on spine, reading
downwards: THE PLACE OF LOVE KARL SHAPIRO. Printed
in green on back cover: A COMMENT / PUBLICATION.

*Note: I was in the army stationed in Australia, which
is where I saw Cecily Crozier's magazine* A Comment *in
a bookstore. I thought it was interesting, so I got
in touch with her and we became good friends. Later,
we decided to put the book together. Some of it came
from letters I wrote her. We lost touch during the
later war years, and I never was able to find out what
happened to her or the books.*

A3 PERSON PLACE AND THING   1942

(a) *First edition:*

[in black:] KARL JAY SHAPIRO / [in blue:] PERSON /
PLACE / AND THING / [in black:] REYNAL & HITCHCOCK

Collation: pp. [i-vi] vii-viii [1-2] 3-32 [33-34] 35-
60 [61-62] 63-88; 9" x 6 1/4"; printed on wove paper.

Pagination: p. [i] half-title, p. [ii] blank, p. [iii]
title page, p. [iv] copyright, acknowledgments, p. [v]
dedication, p. [vi] EDITOR'S NOTE / The selecting,
editing and publishing of / the poems in this volume
have been / done without the author's assistance. /
E [velyn] K [atz], pp. vii-viii CONTENTS, p. [1] section number, p. [2] blank, pp. 3-32 text, p. [33] section number, p. [34] blank, pp. 35-60 text, p. [61]
section number, p. [62] blank, pp. 63-88 text.

Binding: Cream colored cloth over boards. Blue paper
label pasted on spine: [in white:] SHAPIRO / PERSON /
PLACE / AND / THING / REYNAL & / HITCHCOCK. White
endpapers.

Dust jacket: Issued in blue dust jacket with white band
around top and bottom. Front and back: [in black:]
KARL JAY SHAPIRO / [in white:] PERSON / PLACE / AND /
THING / [in black:] REYNAL & HITCHCOCK. Spine: [in
black:] SHAPIRO / [in white:] PERSON, PLACE AND THING
/ [in black:] REYNAL & HITCHCOCK. Flyleaves are white;
front: note on book and K.S.; back: note on book

and K.S. continued.

Publication: Published by Reynal & Hitchcock, November 27, 1942, at $2.50.

Contents: 3 "Scyros," 5 "Necropolis," 6 "The Dome of Sunday," 8 "Property," 10 "Buick," 12 "To a Guineapig," 13 "Epitaph for John and Richard," 14 "Construction," 15 "& Co.," 16 "October 1," 18 "My Grandmother," 19 "Travelogue for Exiles," 20 "Love Poem," 22 "Death of Emma Goldman," 24 "Conscription Camp," 27 "The Twins," 28 "Giantess," 29 "Blindmen," 30 "Elegy for Two Banjos," 32 "Israfel," 35 "Emporium," 36 "University," 38 "Washington Cathedral," 40 "Alexandria," 42 "The Snob," 43 "The Glutton," 44 "Hospital," 46 "Mongolian Idiot," 47 "Waitress," 48 "Midnight Show," 50 "Hollywood," 52 "Auto Wreck," 54 "Honkytonk," 56 "The Fly," 58 "Terminal," 60 "Drug Store," 63 "The Contraband," 64 "Nostalgia," 65 "A Cut Flower," 66 "Barter," 67 "Self-History," 68 "Paradox: The Birds," 69 "Haircut," 70 "How Long Ago the Home," 71 "Elegy Written on a Frontporch," 74 "To Evelyn for Christmas," 75 "Ode for Clenched Teeth," 76 "Druid Hill Park," 80 "Six Religious Lyrics," 84 "A Robbery," 86 "Poet."

Note: When I was in the army during the war I didn't have correspondence with publishers. Evelyn Katz who lived in New York handled all that. I was in the New Directions book Five Young American Poets, *and Albert Erskin was an editor there. Later on, he went to Reynal & Hitchcock, and after that to Random House. That's how I ended up there. Erskin has been the editor of almost all my books, and he was Faulkner's editor. My English editions must have been arranged by him also. I didn't have that kind of clout from the South Pacific.*

(b) *Variant binding:*   1942

Title page, Collation, Pagination, Publication, & Contents same as A3a, save measures 8 1/4" x 5 1/2", & published at $2.00.

Binding: Light gray cloth over boards. Stamped in blue on spine, reading downwards: SHAPIRO PERSON, PLACE AND THING / REYNAL & / HITCHCOCK. White endpapers.

(c) *First English edition:*   1944

KARL JAY SHAPIRO / PERSON, PLACE / AND THING / *London* / SECKER & WARBURG / 1944

Collation: pp. [1-4] 5-63 [64]; 8 3/4" x 5 5/8"; printed on wove paper.

Pagination: p. [1] half-title, p. [2] dedication, p. [3] title page, p. [4] copyright, acknowledgments, AMERICAN EDITOR'S NOTE, pp. 5-6 CONTENTS, pp. 7-[64] text.

Binding: Blue cloth over boards. White endpapers. Issued in dust jacket [unexamined].

Publication: Published at 6s by Secker & Warburg, Ltd., 22 Essex Street, Strand, W.W.2, in January, 1944. Reprinted May, 1944, as indicated on p. [4]. Printed by the Camelot Press Limited, London and Southampton.

Contents: As A3a.

A4 V-LETTER AND OTHER POEMS   1944

[in black:] KARL SHAPIRO / V- / [in red:] LETTER / [in black:] AND OTHER POEMS / REYNAL & HITCHCOCK, NEW YORK

Collation: pp. [i-v] vi-viii [1-2] 3-63 [64]; 8" x 5 1/2"; printed on wove paper.

Pagination: p. [i] half-title, p. [ii] "Also by Karl Shapiro / PERSON, PLACE AND THING," p. [iii] title page, p. [iv] copyright, acknowledgments, p. [v] dedication, p. vi INTRODUCTION, p. vii INTRODUCTION

[continued], "EDITOR'S NOTE / Because for the last
twenty-six months the author has been on / active duty
in the southwest Pacific area, where all of these poems
/ except 'Satire: Anxiety' were written, the selecting,
editing and / arranging of them for this volume have
been done without his / direction. / EVELYN KATZ,"
p. viii CONTENTS, p. [1] half-title, p. [2] blank, pp.
3-63 text, p. [64] blank.

Binding: Light gray cloth over boards. Stamped on
front cover: [in black:] V- / [in red:] LETTER. Stamped
on spine, reading downwards: [in black:] SHAPIRO V-
[in red:] LETTER [in black:] Reynal & / Hitchcock.
White endpapers.

Dust jacket: Issued in gray dust jacket. Front: [in
black:] V- / [in red:] LETTER / [in black:] AND OTHER
POEMS / BY KARL SHAPIRO. Spine, reading downwards:
[in black:] SHAPIRO V- [in red:] LETTER / [in black:]
REYNAL & / HITCHCOCK. Front flyleaf: $2.00 / V-LETTER
/ AND OTHER POEMS / BY KARL SHAPIRO / [from introduction by K.S., and note on A3a] / REYNAL & HITCHCOCK,
INC. / 386 FOURTH AVE., NEW YORK 16, N.Y. Back flyleaf: [from reviews of A3a; ad for *Moderate Fable*
by Marguerite Young; publisher's address].

Publication: Published by Reynal & Hitchcock, August
14, 1944, at $2.00. Printed by the Cornwall Press,
Cornwall, New York.

Contents: 3 "Aside," 5 "Hill at Parramatta," 6 "Melbourne," 7 "Sydney Bridge," 8 "Troop Train," 9 "Christmas Eve: Australia," 10 "New Guinea," 12 "The Gun,"
13 "Sunday: New Guinea," 14 "Fireworks," 15 "Movie
Actress," 16 "Nigger," 18 "Piano," 19 "Jefferson," 20
"Christmas Tree," 21 "Franklin," 22 "The Interlude,"
24 "The Geographers," 25 "The Bed," 26 "Public Library,"
27 "Jew," 28 "Shylock," 29 "Red Indian," 30 "The
Synagogue," 32 "Birthday Poem," 34 "Descent," 35 "Full
Moon: New Guinea," 36 "The Communist," 37 "Lord, I Have
Seen Too Much," 38 "The Leg," 39 "Ballet Mecanique,"
40 "Movie," 42 "Elegy for a Dead Soldier," 47 "D.H.L.,"
48 "The Saint," 49 "Crusoe," 50 "The Puritan," 51 "On

*Notes: The introduction to A4 follows: "All of the
poems in the following pages with a few exceptions
were written in Australia and New Guinea, under the pe-
culiarly enlivening circumstances of soldiering.*

*"Since the war began, I have tried to be on guard
against becoming a 'war poet.' I remember reviewing
some works of certain of the Georgian writers during
my first weeks in the army; at the time I was shocked
to discover that there were men whose recollections
of an old war remained the most cogent experiences of
their lives. A year later, ten thousand miles from
home, I understood better what it was they persisted
in reliving and rewriting: the comparison of the old
peace with the old war seemed to be the expression of
their fate rather than their wish.*

*"There is no need to discuss the private psycho-
logical tragedy of a soldier. It is not the common-
place of suffering or the platitudinous comparison
with the peace, or the focus on the future that should
occupy us; but the spiritual progress or retrogression
of the man in war, the increase or decrease in his
knowledge of beauty, government and religion.*

*"We know very well that the most resounding slogans
ring dead after a few years, and that it is not for
poetry to keep pace with public speeches and the strat-
egy of events. We learn that war is an affection of
the human spirit, without any particular reference to
'values.' In the totality of striving and suffering
we come to see the great configuration abstractly,
with oneself at the center reduced in size but not in
meaning, like a V-letter. We learn that distances and
new spatial arrangements cannot disturb the primordial
equation of man equals man and nation nation. We learn
finally that if war can teach anything it can teach
humility; if it can test anything it can test extern-
ality against the soul.*

*"I have not written these poems to accord with any
doctrine or system of thought or even a theory of*

composition. I have nothing to offer in the way of
beliefs or challenges or prosody. I try to write
freely, one day as a Christian, the next as a Jew,
the next as a soldier who sees the gigantic slapstick
of modern war. I hope I do not impersonate other poets.
Certainly our contemporary man should feel divested of
the stock attitudes of the last generation, the stance
of the political intellectual, the proletarian, the
expert, the salesman, the world traveler, the pundit-
poet. Like the jaded king in the fairy tale we should
find our clothes too delicately spun for the eye to
see; like the youngster in the crowd make the marvel-
lous discovery that our majesty is naked!"

According to Karl Shapiro: "Around the time V-Letter
was published, I was back in the United States. During
the war they had a point system--if you were overseas
so many years you'd build up enough points to be sent
back. Because I was one of the first soldiers to go
overseas, I was sent back before the war was over.
While I was staying with Evelyn in her New York apartment, Louis Untermeyer telephoned me and said that although it was a secret, I was going to win the Pulitzer
Prize. He was on the committee and he spilled the
beans. It was very exciting. About this time I asked
for a transfer out of the medical corps and into the
OSS, the spy organization. I had met Selden Rodman,
the poet and critic, in Washington; he was working
for the OSS and wanted me to move over there. I stayed
until my discharge came through, then I told them I
wanted to quit. They got pretty upset. People weren't
supposed to leave that organization."

A5   ESSAY ON RIME   1945

(a) *First edition:*

[in black:] ESSAY ON / [in red:] RIME / [in black:] BY
KARL SHAPIRO / REYNAL & HITCHCOCK, NEW YORK

Collation: pp. [i-viii] 1-3 [4-6] 7-24 [25-26] 27-48

[49-50] 51-60 [70] 71-72; 8" x 5 1/2"; printed on
wove paper.

Pagination: p. [i] half-title, p. [ii] BOOKS BY KARL
SHAPIRO: / PERSON, PLACE AND THING / V-LETTER AND
OTHER POEMS / ESSAY ON RIME, p. [iii] title page, p.
[iv] acknowledgments, copyright, printer's address,
p. [v] dedication, p. [vi] blank, p. [vii] CONTENTS,
p. [viii] blank, pp. 1-3 FOREWORD, p. [4] blank, p.
[5] THE CONFUSION / IN PROSODY / 1, p. [6] blank, pp.
7-24 text, p. [25] THE CONFUSION / IN LANGUAGE / 2,
p. [26] blank, pp. 27-48 text, p. [49] THE CONFUSION
/ IN BELIEF / 3, p. [50] blank, pp. 51-69 text, p.
[70] blank, pp. 71-72 NOTE AND ACKNOWLEDGMENT.

Binding: Light gray cloth over boards. Stamped on
front cover: [in black:] ESSAY ON [in red:] RIME.
Stamped on spine: [in black:] ESSAY ON [in red:]
RIME [in black:] BY KARL SHAPIRO / REYNAL & / HITCHCOCK.
White endpapers.

Dust jacket: Issued in dust jacket. Front cover &
spine, red paper. Front: [in black:] ESSAY ON / [in
white:] RIME / [in black:] KARL SHAPIRO. Spine, reading downwards: [in black:] ESSAY ON [in white:] RIME
[in black:] BY KARL SHAPIRO / REYNAL & / HITCHCOCK.
Back cover & flyleaves, white paper. Front flyleaf
and back cover contain quotes from a review of A5a
by F.O. Matthiessen in the *New York Times Book Review*;
back flyleaf contains ads for A3a, A4.

Publication: Published by Reynal & Hitchcock, October
29, 1945, at $2.00. Printed by the Cornwall Press,
Cornwall, New York.

Contents: "Essay on Rime."

*Note: We were once told that my outfit had a ninety-
day rest period because we were then going to move
farther up into the island. I was the company clerk
so I had a typewriter, and I decided that since I
had ninety days with nothing to do I'd write this
poem* ["Essay on Rime"]. *I wish I still had the notes*

to the thing. *I actually sat down and blocked out the poem I wanted to write; I divided it into sections, gave them titles, and even figured out how many lines a day I'd be able to write. And then I wrote about thirty lines a day for ninety days. I never really thought the poem would be published. I didn't even have any books with me when I wrote it. One guy claimed there was a library in the port I was at in New Guinea, and it turns out there was—but I didn't know about it at the time. William Van O'Connor was stationed there also, and he came to see me after hearing I had won some prize. He loaned me his copy of Yeats' anthology of modern verse, and I had my own copy of Baudelaire. That was about the extent of my library at that time. It really wasn't hard to write that kind of poem. I had an idea of what I wanted to say and that was that.*

(b) *First English edition:*   1947

ESSAY ON / RIME / *BY KARL SHAPIRO* / London [slanted rule] SECKER & WARBURG [slanted rule] 1947

Collation: pp. [1-6] 7-9 [10] 11-64; 8 3/4" x 5 3/4"; printed on wove paper.

Pagination: p. [1] half-title, p. [2] books by K.S., p. [3] title page, p. [4] acknowledgments, dedication, publisher's address, printer, p. [5] CONTENTS, p. [6] blank, pp. 7-9 FOREWORD, p. [10] blank, pp. 11-64 text.

Binding: Light gray cloth over boards. Spine, reading downwards, in gold: *ESSAY ON RIME* [device] *KARL SHA-PIRO S&W*. White endpapers.

Dust jacket: Issued in dust jacket [unexamined].

Publication: Published by Martin Secker & Warburg, Ltd., 7 John St., London, W.C.1, in January, 1947, at 6*s*. Printed by the Camelot Press, Ltd., London and Southampton.

Contents: As A5a.

(c) *First Random House edition:*   [1958]

Title page, Collation, Pagination, & Contents as A5a,
save title page is in black, [ii] adds *Trial of a Poet
/ Poems 1940-53 / Beyond Criticism / Poems of a Jew /
In Defense of Ignorance,* [iv] acknowledgments and
printer's address dropped.

Binding: Spine of A5a is beveled; spine of A5c is not.
Spine, reading downwards: ESSAY ON RIME BY KARL SHA-
PIRO RANDOM HOUSE.

Dust jacket: As A5a, save spine reads RANDOM HOUSE;
also, back flyleaf contains ads for books as above.

Publication: Published by Random House at $3.00 in
[1958].

A6   ENGLISH PROSODY AND MODERN POETRY   1947

ENGLISH PRODOSY AND / MODERN POETRY / BY / KARL SHAPIRO
/ 1947 / THE JOHNS HOPKINS PRESS / BALTIMORE 18, MARY-
LAND

Collation: pp. [i-iv] 1-16; 9" x 6"; Printed on wove
paper.

Pagination: p. [1] title page, p. [ii] Reprinted from
ELH, A Journal of English Literary History, / Volume
Fourteen, Number Two, June, 1947, p. [iii] IN MEMORY
OF DOCTOR HAZELTON SPENCER / CRITIC AND FRIEND, p.
[iv] blank, pp. 1-16 text.

Binding: Issued in light gray paper covers, stapled.
Front cover: ENGLISH PROSODY AND / MODERN POETRY /
BY / KARL SHAPIRO.

Publication: Published as a reprint from *ELH, A Journal
of English Literary History,* XIV, 2, by The Johns Hopkins University Press, June, 1947, at 50¢.

Contents: "English Prosody and Modern Poetry."

Notes: This essay was delivered April 18, 1947, by K.S. as the annual Tudor and Stuart Club Lecture. In 1973, Folcroft Publishing Company reprinted A6 in a library binding at $6.50. In 1977, Norwood Editions reprinted an unauthorized edition of A6 at $6.00.

This was a transcription of a lecture I gave at Hopkins to get a job. I knew my job at the Library of Congress was ending, and I needed work. They gave me an associate professorship with tenure right off the bat. It was pretty funny.

A7 TRIAL OF A POET   1947

(a) *First edition:*

KARL SHAPIRO / TRIAL / OF A POET / AND OTHER POEMS / REYNAL & HITCHCOCK, NEW YORK

Collation: pp. [i-xiv] [1-2] 3-22 [23-24] 25-52 [53-56] 57-81 [82]; 8" x 5 1/2"; printed on wove paper.

Pagination: pp. [i-ii] blank, p. [iii] half-title, p. [iv] blank, p. [v] list of books by K.S., p. [vi] blank, p. [vii] title page, p. [viii] copyright, p. [ix] acknowledgments, p. [x] blank, p. [xi] dedication, p. [xii] blank, p. [xiii] contents, p. [xiv] blank, p. [1] "Recapitulations," p. [2] blank, pp. 3-22 text, p. [23] "The Progress of Faust," p. [24] blank, pp. 25-52 text, p. [53] "Trial of a Poet," p. [54] blank, p. [55] "In seeking just occasion to provoke / The *Philistine*, thy Countries Enemy, / Thou never wast remiss, I bear thee witness: / Yet *Israel* serves with all his sons. / Milton," pp. [56]-81 text, p. [82] blank.

Binding: Gray cloth over boards. Stamped in red on spine, reading downwards: Karl Shapiro TRIAL OF A POET / REYNAL & / HITCHCOCK. White endpapers.

Dust jacket: Issued in dust jacket. Front cover and
spine, paper in gray. Front: [in white:] KARL SHAPIRO
/ [in red:] TRIAL / [in white:] OF A [in red:] POET.
Spine, reading downwards: [in white:] Karl Shapiro
[in red:] TRIAL [in white:] OF A [in red:] POET [in
white:] Reynal & / Hitchcock. Back cover and flyleaves, white paper printed in red and gray. Back
cover advertises "DISTINGUISHED POETRY" published by
Reynal & Hitchcock, including books by Henry Reed,
Richard Wilbur, Denis Devlin, Weldon Kees, and Reed
Whittemore.

Publication: Published by Reynal & Hitchcock, October
29, 1947, at $2.00. Printed by the Cornwall Press,
Cornwall, New York.

Contents: 1 "Recapitulations," 25 "Homecoming," 27
"The Voyage," 28 "Demobilization," 30 "The Conscientious Objector," 32 "An Urn of Ashes," 34 "In the
Waxworks," 36 "The Southerner," 38 "D.C.," 40 "Boy-
Man," 42 "The Aunt," 43 "Air Liner," 45 "The New Ring,"
46 "The Dirty Word," 47 "Words for a Child's Birthday,"
49 "The Convert," 51 "The Progress of Faust," 53 "Trial
of a Poet."

*Note: Some of these poems were written while I was in
the Pacific, some on the way home, and some in New
York. It's possible I had something to do with the
actual publication of this book because when I got
back to the States one of the first things I did was
to go see people at Reynal & Hitchcock. There was a
limited edition of the thing, signed and so forth.
I don't really understand the point of limited editions
--they seem like a kind of self-important thing to do.
But publishers like them.*

(b) *Limited edition:*   1947

Title, Collation, Pagination, & Contents as A7a, save
p. [1] reads "Two hundred and fifty copies of the /
first edition of TRIAL OF A POET / have been printed
on a special rag / content paper of which this is

Poems

Karl Jay Shapiro

Baltimore, Maryland
1935

A1

KARL SHAPIRO

V-
LETTER

AND OTHER POEMS

REYNAL & HITCHCOCK, NEW YORK

A4

A BIBLIOGRAPHY OF MODERN PROSODY

By KARL SHAPIRO
THE CHAIR OF POETRY
THE LIBRARY OF CONGRESS
1946-1947

BALTIMORE
THE JOHNS HOPKINS PRESS
1948

A8

THE
BOURGEOIS
POET

Karl Shapiro

RANDOM HOUSE   NEW YORK

A13

copy / number [187] / [signature of K.S. in gray ink]."

Binding: Front and back covers, gray cloth over boards.
Spine, blue cloth over boards. Cream colored label
pasted on spine, lettered in red: SHAPIRO / TRIAL /
OF A / POET / REYNAL & / HITCHCOCK. White endpapers.

Publication: Published by Reynal & Hitchcock, October
29, 1947, in a signed edition limited to 250 numbered
copies at $5.00.

A8   A BIBLIOGRAPHY OF MODERN PROSODY   1948

A BIBLIOGRAPHY OF / MODERN PROSODY / By KARL SHAPIRO
/ THE CHAIR OF POETRY / The Library of Congress / 1946-
1947 / [publisher's emblem] / BALTIMORE / THE JOHNS
HOPKINS PRESS / 1948

Collation: pp. [i-iv] 1-31 [32] 33-36; 8 1/2" x 5 1/2";
printed on wove paper.

Pagination: p. [1] half-title, p. [ii] LONDON: GEOFFREY
CUMBRLEGE / OXFORD UNIVERSITY PRESS, p. [iii] title
page, p. [iv] printer's statement, pp. 1-4 INTRODUC-
TION, pp. 5-31 text, p. [32] blank, pp. 33-36 GLOSSARY.
White endpapers.

Binding: Gray cloth over boards, stamped in gold on
front cover and spine. Front: A BIBLIOGRAPHY OF /
MODERN PROSODY / [rule] / SHAPIRO / [publisher's
emblem]. Spine: [decorative rule] SHAPIRO: A BIBLI-
OGRAPHY OF MODERN PROSODY [decorative rule].

Dust jacket: Issued in dust jacket [unexamined].

Publication: Published by The Johns Hopkins University
Press in 1948 at $1.75. Printed by Oxford University
Press, London.

Contents: An annotated list of seventy-one books and
articles on modern prosody, with glossary.

Notes: In 1973, Folcroft Publishing Company reprinted A8 in library binding at $6.50. In 1977, Norwood Editions reprinted an unauthorized edition of A8 at $6.00.

I did this bibliography when I was still working at the Library of Congress. Nobody knew exactly what my job was supposed to be, and someone suggested that I do a bibliography on something as they had all the books. It really wasn't very extensive.

A9   POEMS 1940-1953   1953

POEMS / 1940-1953 / KARL SHAPIRO / [publisher's emblem] / RANDOM HOUSE / NEW YORK

Collation: pp. [i-xii] [1-2] 3-159 [160] 161 [162-164]; 9 1/4" x 8 7/8"; printed on wove paper.

Pagination: pp. [i-ii] blank, p. [iii] half title, p. [iv] "Also / by / Karl / Shapiro: / Person, Place and Thing / V-Letter and Other Poems / Essay on Rime / Trial of a Poet," p. [v] title page, p. [vi] copyright, acknowledgment, p. [vii] dedication, p. [viii] blank, pp. [ix-xii] contents, p. [1] half-title, p. [2] blank, pp. 3-159 text, p. [160] blank, p. 161 "About the Author," pp. [162-164] blank.

Dust jacket: Issued in dust jacket. Front cover and spine: gray with white printing, yellow rule across center. Front: POEMS / 1940-1953 / [yellow rule] / Karl Shapiro / A RANDOM HOUSE BOOK [publisher's emblem]. Spine: POEMS / 1940 / 1953 / [yellow rule] / Karl Shapiro RANDOM HOUSE. Back and front flyleaves: white paper, printed in black. Back cover: "Karl Shapiro was born in Baltimore, Mary- / land, on November 10, 1913, and was educated at the Uni- / versity of Virginia and at Johns Hopkins University. When / his first book, *Person, Place and Thing*, was published in 1942, / Mr. Shapiro was already with the army in the South Pacific, / where he remained until the spring

of 1945. In 1946 he was / appointed as Consultant in
Poetry at the Library Of Congress, / and then, in 1947,
to the faculty of Johns Hopkins University, / where
he taught writing courses until he resigned in 1950 to
/ become Editor of *Poetry: A Magazine of Verse.* / The
second and third of Mr. Shapiro's books--*V-Letter and
/ Other Poems*, which was awarded the Pulitzer Prize
in 1945, / and *Essay On Rime*--were also published
while he was on / duty in the South Pacific. The
fourth and most recent volume, / *Trial of a Poet*,
appeared in 1947. / During the years from 1940 to
1953 his poems, essays and / reviews have appeared in
leading literary magazines all over / the world."
Front flyleaf: $4.50 / POEMS / 1940-1953 / [yellow
rule] / by Karl Shapiro / This volume, which contains
106 / poems in all, represents the author's own /
choice from the contents of three previ- / ously
published collections--*Person, Place / and Thing, V-
Letter and Other Poems* / (Pulitzer Prize, 1945), and
Trial of a Poet / --and eighteen more recent poems
that / have not appeared before in book form.

Binding: Black cloth over boards. Publisher's emblem
blind-stamped on lower right corner of front cover.
Gold stamped on spine: POEMS 1940-1953 by Karl Shapiro
RANDOM HOUSE. White endpapers.

Publication: Published by Random House, New York,
September 15, 1953, at $4.00. Designed by Ernst Reichl.

Contents: 3 "Adam and Eve," 13 "Auto Wreck," 15 "Ballet
Mecanique," 16 "The Bed," 17 "Birthday Poem," 19 "Blind-
man," 22 "Buick," 24 "A Calder," 25 "Carte Postale,"
26 "The Conscientious Objector," 28 "Construction,"
29 "The Contraband," 30 "Conscription Camp," 32 "A Cut
Flower," 33 "D.C.," 34 "Death of Emma Goldman," 35
"The Dirty Word," 36 "The Dome of Sunday," 38 "Drug
Store," 39 "Druid Hill Park," 41 "Ego," 42 "Elegy for
a Dead Soldier," 47 "Elegy for Two Banjos," 49 "Elegy
Written on a Frontporch," 52 "Emporium," 53 "Epitaph
for John and Richard," 54 "The Figurehead," 55 "Fireworks," 56 "The Fly," 58 "F.O. Matthiessen: An Anniversary," 60 "Franklin," 61 "Full Moon: New Guinea," 62

"Giantess," 63 "Glass Poem," 64 "The Glutton," 65 "Going to School," 68 "Guineapig," 69 "The Gun," 70 "Haircut," 71 "Hill at Parramatta," 72 "Hollywood," 74
"Homecoming," 76 "Honkytonk," 78 "Hospital," 80 "The
Intellectual," 82 "The Interlude," 85 "In the Waxworks,"
87 "Israel," 88 "Israfel," 89 "Jefferson," 90 "The Leg,"
91 "Lord, I Have Seen Too Much," 92 "Love for a Hand,"
93 "Magician," 95 "Melbourne," 96 "Midnight Show," 98
"The Minute," 99 "Mongolian Idiot," 100 "My Grandmother," 101 "Necropolis," 102 "The New Ring," 103
"Nigger," 105 "Nostalgia," 106 "October 1," 108 "The
Phenomenon," 109 "Piano," 110 "Poet," 113 "The Potomac,"
114 "The Progress of Faust," 116 "Recapitulations,"
122 "Red Indian," 123 "A Robbery," 125 "Satire: Anxiety," 127 "Scyros," 129 "The Second-Best Bed," 131
"Six Religious Lyrics," 137 "The Snob," 138 "The Southerner," 140 "Sydney Bridge," 141 "The Synagogue," 143
"Terminal," 145 "The Tingling Back," 147 "To Evelyn
for Christmas," 148 "Travelogue for Exiles," 149 "Troop
Train," 151 "The Twins," 152 "University," 154 "V-
Letter," 156 "The Voyage," 157 "Waitress," 158 "Washington Cathedral."

A10 BEYOND CRITICISM   1953

(a) *First edition:*

[in black:] *Karl Shapiro* / [in brown:] Beyond Criticism
/ [in black:] What the Poet Knows / The True Artificer
/ The Career of the Poem / [rule] / *The University of
Nebraska Press*

Collation: pp. [i-viii] 1-73 [74-76]; 8 1/2" x 5 1/2";
printed on wove paper.

Pagination: pp. [i-ii] blank, p. [iii] title page, p.
[iv] copyright, p. [v] contents, p. [vi] "The original
title of the work which constitutes the / Montgomery
Lectureship on Contemporary Civilization, 1953, was: /
A PRIMER FOR POETS / My thanks are due to Professor
Julius Cohen of the College of Law, University of

Nebraska, for suggesting the present title," p. [vii]
"Man has to realize personality. / Personality is
spirit, free spirit / and the link between man and
God. / It is a link of man with God which / is outside
objectivisation, and out- / side the false submergence
of man in / his own closed circle. Through it / is
revealed infinity and eternity and / authentic beauty.
/ Nicholas Berdyaev / *Slavery and Freedom*," p. [viii]
blank, pp. 1-73 text, pp. [74-76] blank.

Binding: Issued in reddish brown cloth. Stamped in
silver on front cover: Beyond / Criticism. Stamped in
silver on spine, reading downwards: BEYOND CRITICISM
KARL SHAPIRO NEBRASKA.

Dust jacket: Issued in dust jacket [unexamined].

Publication: Published by the University of Nebraska
Press, September 14, 1953, at $3.00.

Contents: 1 "Introduction," 7 "What The Poet Knows,"
29 "The True Artificer," 51 "The Career of the Poem."

(b) *First paper edition:*   1953

[in black:] MONTGOMERY LECTURESHIP / ON CONTEMPORARY
CIVILIZATION / [rule] / BEYOND CRITICISM / [in brown:]
Karl Shapiro / [in black:] Introduction / What the
poet knows / The true artificer / The career of the
poem / [rule] / PUBLISHED BY / THE UNIVERSITY OF
NEBRASKA / AT LINCOLN, 1953.

Collation, Pagination, Publication, & Contents as
A10a, save measures 8" x 5 1/4".

Binding: Issued in white paper wrappers, stapled.
Front cover: [in black:] 1953 / MONTGOMERY LECTURE-
SHIP / ON CONTEMPORARY CIVILIZATION / [in brown:]
Karl Shapiro / [in black:] BEYOND CRITICISM / [in
brown: rule] / [in black:] THE UNIVERSITY OF NEBRASKA.
Brown rule extends across spine and back cover.

(c) *Second paper edition* [*A Primer for Poets*]: 1965

A PRIMER FOR POETS / Karl Shapiro / [publisher's emblem] / A / BISON / BOOK / UNIVERSITY OF NEBRASKA PRESS [device] Lincoln

Collation: pp. [i-iv] v-vi [vii-x] 1-73 [74]; 8" x 5 3/8"; printed on wove paper.

Pagination: pp. [i-ii] blank, p. [iii] title page, p. [iv] copyright, "*This book originally was published under the title* Beyond Criticism," pp. v-vi "FOREWORD TO THE / BISON BOOK EDITION," p. [vii] contents, p. [viii] blank, p. [ix] half-title, p. [x] blank, pp. 1-73 text, p. [74] blank.

Binding: Issued in stiff paper covers. Front cover: [in blue:] A / PRIMER / FOR / POETS / [in black:] KARL SHAPIRO / THREE ESSAYS: [in green:] What the poet knows / The true artificer / The career of the poem / [in black: publisher's emblem] / $1.00. Spine, reading downwards: SHAPIRO *A PRIMER FOR POETS* BB 307. Back cover: Selections from reviews of A10a. Designed by Jerry Graff.

Publication: Published by the University of Nebraska Press as a Bison Book at $1.00 in 1965.

Contents: As A10a; adds "Foreword to the Bison Book Edition," v-vi.

Note: Restores original title to the Montgomery Lectureship on Contemporary Civilization given in 1953 by K.S. at the University of Nebraska. According to K.S. in the Foreword to A10c, "*These essays, written more than a decade ago, were my first attempt to say no to Criticism. Logically to say no to Criticism means to abstain from reading or writing it. It means to create or trying to create in an atmosphere in which nothing seems to take root except Criticism. It means to walk out of the lecture hall, where these lectures were given. Stop lecturing, for God's sake! is what these lectures say.*"

A11 POEMS OF A JEW   1958

BY KARL SHAPIRO / Poems of a Jew / [publisher's emblem]
RANDOM HOUSE NEW YORK

Collation: pp. [i-viii] ix-xi [xii-xiv] [1-2] 3-19 [20-
22] 23-46 [47-48] 49-70 [71-74]; 9" x 6"; printed on
wove paper.

Pagination: p. [i] half-title, p. [ii] "by Karl Shapiro
PERSON, PLACE AND THING / V-LETTER AND OTHER POEMS /
ESSAY ON RIME / TRIAL OF A POET / POEMS 1940-1953 /
POEMS OF A JEW," p. [iii] title page, p. [iv] copyright,
acknowledgments, p. [v] dedication, p. [vi] blank, p.
[vii] contents, p. [viii] blank, pp. ix-xi Introduction,
p. [xii] blank, p. [xiii] "branding instead of beauty
/ DEAD SEA SCROLLS," p. [xiv] blank, p. [1] "PART 1,"
p. [2] blank, pp. 3-19 text, p. [20] blank, p. [21]
"PART 2," p. [22] blank, pp. 23-46 text, p. [47] "PART
3," p. [48] blank, pp. 49-71 text, p. [72] blank, p.
[73] "ABOUT THE AUTHOR," p. [74] blank.

Binding: Black cloth over boards. Stamped in red on
front cover: Poems of a Jew. Spine: [in silver:]
POEMS OF A JEW [in red:] by Karl Shapiro [in silver:]
RANDOM HOUSE.

Dust jacket: Issued in dust jacket. Front cover and
spine, light yellow paper. Front: [in red:] P [in
black:] oems / of a / Jew / by [in red:] karl shapiro
/ [in black:] A RANDOM HOUSE BOOK. Spine, reading
downwards: [in black:] Poems of a Jew [in red:] karl
shapiro [in black: publisher's emblem] random house.
Back cover and flyleaves, white paper printed in black;
back contains photograph of the author taken by Evelyn
Shapiro, with note on Shapiro's life; front flyleaf:
a selection from author's introduction; back flyleaf:
ads for other Shapiro books with critical comment.
Jacket designed by Clifton Lane.

Publication: Published by Random House, New York, May
12, 1958, at $3.50.

Contents: ix-xi Introduction, 3 "The Alphabet," 4
"Israel," 5 "The Dirty Word," 6 "The 151st Psalm," 7
"The Olive Tree," 8 "The Synagogue," 11 "The Phenome-
non," 12 "University," 14 "Washington Cathedral," 16
"The Tingling Back," 18 "Travelogue for Exiles," 19
"Lord, I Have Seen Too Much," 23 "Messias," 25 "The
Confirmation," 27 "The Jew at Christmas Eve," 28 "The
First Time," 30 "Christmas Eve: Australia," 31 "Sunday:
New Guinea," 32 "The Leg," 34 "Five Self-Portraits,"
39 "V-Letter," 42 "The Ham-Bone of a Saint," 45 "Teasing the Nuns," 46 "The Crucifix in the Filing Cabinet,"
49 "My Grandmother," 50 "Jew," 51 "The Southerner,"
53 "The Murder of Moses," 55 "Shylock," 57 "The Progress of Faust," 59 "Mongolian Idiot," 60 "The Convert,"
62 "Adam and Eve," 70 Notes.

*Note: At this time I really didn't have any Jewish
affiliations. My wife's father was an atheist and a
Marxist, so there was no pressure on that score.
There just seemed to be something in my own consciousness that I wanted to articulate. It's something that
never really goes away. When the Jews are not in
trouble, I forget about the whole thing. Then something happens, like trouble in Israel, and it comes
back at me. In this book* [Poems of a Jew] *I was trying to do something like Alfred Kazin is doing in the
second volume of his autobiography,* New York Jew.
*"New York Jew" has bad connotations, and I think I
understand them. When I was a kid starting to write,
you could tell that the poetry establishment in this
country was WASP by looking in the poetry anthologies.
There was one guy named James Oppenheimer who wrote
in the Whitman style; he wasn't that great a poet,
but most of his poems were about Hebrews and the
Bible. He was the only Jewish writer I knew about.
I really believed that it was very hard to get published if you didn't have a WASP name, and in a sense
that was true. As Kazin points out in his book, the
first Jew to be hired in the English Department at
Columbia was Lionel Trilling! That was a shock to
the whole academic community in the United States, a
blockbuster. Imagine letting a Jew into an English
Department! Something along the same line happened*

to me. *I was the second Jew to be hired at Johns Hopkins, and a good friend of mine was the first Jew to
get a Ph.D. at Hopkins. This is recent history! But
now of course the Jews practically run the place.*

*Anyway, because of all this, I toyed with the
idea of taking an English name. There was a beautiful
old railroad station in Baltimore called Camden Station
--it was the place the first shots of the Civil War
were fired. I was going to change my name to Karl
Camden. I knew a lot of Jews who did that. In fact,
while many of the Jews writing today don't deny their
Jewishness, many of them changed their names early on
to English names. It was very common just after the
war. I didn't do it, however, because I figured my
identity was somehow bound up in my name. If I changed
it, I would be doing something very false, and I couldn't
handle that. One thing I did do when I was a kid was
change my first name from being spelled with a C to a
K. I think one reason for that was that one of my
grandfathers was a German; we were always led to believe that German Jews were better than Russian Jews,
so when I found out that Karl was a German spelling of
my name, I changed it.*

A12   IN DEFENSE OF IGNORANCE   1960

(a) *First edition:*

In / Defense / of / Ignorance / KARL SHAPIRO / [pub-
lisher's emblem] / RANDOM HOUSE / New York

Collation: pp. [i-iv] v-vii [viii] ix-x [xi-xii] [1-
2] 3-33 [34] 35-85 [86] 87-113 [114] 115-141 [142]
143-169 [170] 171-217 [218] 219-261 [262] 263-285
[286] 287-338 [339-340]; 7 1/2" x 4 1/2"; printed on
wove paper.

Pagination: p. [1] half-title, p. [ii] other books by
K.S., p. [iii] title page, p. [iv] copyright, pp. v-vi
acknowledgments, p. vii contents, p. [viii] blank, pp.
ix-x "To The Reader," p. [xi] "everything / we are

taught / is false," p. [xii] blank, p. [1] half-title,
p. [2] blank, pp. 3-33 text, p. [34] blank, pp. 35-85
text, p. [86] blank, pp. 87-113 text, p. [114] blank,
pp. 115-141 text, p. [142] blank, pp. 143-169 text,
p. [170] blank, pp. 171-217 text, p. [218] blank, pp.
219-261 text, p. [262] blank, pp. 263-285, p. [286]
blank, pp. 287-338 text, p. [339] "ABOUT THE AUTHOR,"
p. [340] blank.

Binding: Black cloth over boards. Cover: [gold rule
with KS inset]. Spine: [in silver:] In / Defense /
of / Ignorance / [gold rule:] / [in silver:] KARL
SHAPIRO / [in gold: publisher's emblem] / [in silver:]
RANDOM HOUSE. White endpapers.

Dust jacket: Issued in dust jacket. Front cover: [in
blue:] IN DEFENSE OF / IGNORANCE [in yellow:] BY /
KARL SHAPIRO / [in black:] A distinguished American
poet's first collection of essays. Spine: [in blue:]
IN DEFENSE OF / IGNORANCE [in yellow:] BY / KARL
SHAPIRO / [in black: publisher's emblem] / Random
House. Back cover: [photograph of K.S. by Anthony
Ostroff, note on K.S.]. Front flyleaf: [in blue:]
IN DEFENSE OF / IGNORANCE [in yellow:] BY / KARL
SHAPIRO / [in black: note on book]. Back flyleaf:
[ads for other Shapiro books]. Dust jacket designed
by George Tscherny.

Publication: Published by Random House, New York,
April 14, 1960, at $4.00. Printed by the Haddon
Craftsmen, Scranton, PA.

Contents: ix "To the reader," 3 "The Critic in Spite
of Himself," 35 "T. S. Eliot: The Death of Literary
Judgement," 61 "Ezra Pound: The Scapegoat of Modern
Poetry," 87 "W. B. Yeats: Trial by Culture," 115 "The
Retreat of W. H. Auden," 143 "William Carlos Williams:
The True Contemporary," 171 "Dylan Thomas," 187 "The
First White Aboriginal," 205 "The Jewish Writer in
America," 219 "Poets and Psychologists," 239 "The Un-
employed Magician," 263 "What Is Not Poetry?" 287
"Poets of the Cosmic Consciousness," 313 "The Greatest
Living Author."

Notes: I was at Notre Dame a few weeks ago and one of the professors there said to me, "You don't know what an effect In Defense of Ignorance *had. It really ripped the whole academic community in half." I'm glad I wrote the book, I like it. I think I still stand by my observations, although I wouldn't write it so violently now. I've always been American in the Whitman sense, and the poets who followed that ethos are the poets I feel most comfortable with. All the essays included there were given as lectures at the University of Cincinnati to large audiences. I was there for about a semester, teaching a creative writing class and giving these lectures. The Eliot lecture really caused an uproar. Some of the professors in attendance got up and walked out in the middle of it. And when the piece appeared in the* Saturday Review, *it caused a real stir. I didn't think about it too much, however, for two reasons. First, I have a sort of special status around English departments--I'm not really a professor, but sort of a mad guest. Too, I really wasn't alone in my feelings about Eliot and Modernism. When I was at the University of Nebraska, there was a core of people who felt the way I did. James E. Miller and Bernice Slote shared my point of view. Anyway, I wrote all the lectures in advance except for the Henry Miller piece. I did that one just a couple days before I gave it, while sitting in a beautiful house overlooking a golf course and drinking scotch. I wrote it while I was bombed but it came out the way I wanted it.*

"The Greatest Living Author" was reprinted as a foreword to the Grove Press edition of Henry Miller's *Tropic of Cancer* in 1961.

(b) *First paper edition:*   1965

IN DEFENSE / of IGNORANCE / Karl Shapiro / VINTAGE BOOKS / [publisher's emblem] / A Division of Random House / NEW YORK

Collation, Pagination, & Contents as A12a.

Binding: Issued in stiff paper covers. Front cover:
[in blue:] IN DEFENSE OF / IGNORANCE [in yellow:] BY
/ KARL SHAPIRO / [in black:] A Distinguished American
Poet's First Collection of Essays / [in blue:] A Vin-
tage Book [publisher's emblem] V-275 [in black:] $1.95.
Spine, reading downwards: [in blue:] IN DEFENSE OF
IGNORANCE [in yellow:] BY KARL SHAPIRO / [in blue:
publisher's emblem] / [in black:] VINTAGE / V-275.
Back cover: [in blue:] IN DEFENSE OF IGNORANCE / [in
yellow:] KARL SHAPIRO / [in black: quotations from
reviews of A12a by Robert H. Glauber, John Logan, and
Theodore Solotaroff] / [in blue:] Also available in
a hardcover edition from Random House [in yellow:] A
Vintage Book.

Publication: Published in 1965 by Vintage Books, New
York (Random House / Alfred A. Knopf, Inc.), at $1.95.

A13 THE BOURGEOIS POET   1964

(a) *First edition:*

[rule] / THE / BOURGEOIS / POET / [device] / Karl
Shapiro / [publisher's emblem] / RANDOM HOUSE NEW YORK

Collation: pp. [i-vi] [1-2] 3-47 [48-50] 51-84 [85-
86] 87-120 [121-122]; 8 1/4" x 5 1/2"; printed on
wove paper.

Pagination: p. [i] half-title, p. [ii] other books
by K.S., p. [iii] title page, p. [iv] copyright, p.
[v] "How many precautions are necessary to keep oneself from lying! / [device] / That frightful quantity
of I's and me's / [device] / What! Is it nothing but
that?" / The Life of Henri Brulard, p. [vi] blank, p.
[1] I / The Bourgeois Poet, p. [2] blank, pp. 3-47
text, p. [48] blank, p. [49] II / Doctor Poet, p.
[50] blank, pp. 51-84 text, p. [85] III / End Paper,
p. [86] blank, pp. 87-120 text, p. [121] ABOUT THE

AUTHOR, p. [122] blank.

Binding: Blue cloth over boards, stamped in gold.
Front cover: [device, rule]. Spine, reading downwards: The Bourgeois Poet [device] Karl Shapiro /
[publisher's emblem] / RANDOM HOUSE. White endpapers.

Dust jacket: Issued in dust jacket. Front and back
covers, spine, paper dark blue. Front: [in yellow:]
The / Bourgeois / Poet / [in white: rule] / [in light
blue:] Karl Shapiro. Spine, reading downwards: [in
yellow:] The Bourgeois Poet [in white: rule] [in
light blue:] Karl Shapiro / [in white: publisher's
emblem] / Random House. Back: [photograph of K.S.] /
[in white:] PHOTO: Charles Armstrong / [in yellow:]
KARL SHAPIRO. Flyleaves, paper in white. Front flyleaf: [in blue:] $4.00 / T. B. P. / R. H. / [in black:]
"This is Karl Shapiro's first volume of / poetry since
Poems of a Jew (1958). / All of these new poems are
in a form Mr. Shapiro experimented with occas- / ion-
ally years ago (There are two ex- / amples in *Trial
of a Poet*, 1947) and / which he has been using more
fre- / quently in recent years--a form in / which he
eschews not only rhyme but / versification as well.
It is his belief that / these two traditional attri-
butes of / poetry are nonessential and artificial /
impediments to the poetic process. / [in blue:] 5/64
/ jacket design by Anita Karl. Back flyleaf: [bio-
graphical statement].

Publication: Published by Random House, New York,
April 16, 1964, at $4.00. Printed by the Haddon
Craftsmen, Inc., Scranton, PA. Designed by Terry
LoPrete.

Contents: 3 "The world is my dream," 4 "The look of
shock on an old friend's face," 5 "Oriental, you give
and give," 6 "The rice around the lingam stone," 7
"Of love and death in the Garrison State I sing," 8
"Quintana lay in the shallow grave of coral," 9 "The
bourgeois poet," 9 "Office love," 10 "Lower the standard," 11 "Waiting in front of the columnar high
school," 12 "The cat, outrageously unprepared for

life," 13 "The dermatologist committed suicide," 14
"Italy spoiled California for me," 15 "The password
of the twentieth century," 16 "It's lovely when one
of them," 17 "Abraham Lincoln wore the chimney hat,"
18 "The child who is silent stands against his father,"
19 "One of those idle autumn evenings," 20 "Always
another proverb that contradicts the first one," 20
"Libraries, where one takes on the smell of books,"
21 "The two-year-old has had a motherless week," 22
"All tropic places smell of mold," 23 "From the top
floor of the Tulsa hotel," 24 "There's a Parthenon
in Nashville," 25 "Between the *Times* and *Partisan*,"
26 "Hart Crane, though handicapped, did well," 27 "Why
poetry small and cramped," 28 "Broken bottles hard-set
in cement," 29 "The living rooms of my neighbors are
like beauty parlors," 30 "It happens sometimes in the
best of families," 31 "After a war the boys," 33 "The
History of Philosophy professor is a fashion plate,"
34 "When suffering is everywhere," 34 "I am an athiest
who says his prayers," 51 "This Slavic typist had high
cheekbones," 52 "In the second-best hotel in Tokyo,"
53 "I wait up for the movies of my war," 54 "The poet
takes the voyage to the New Cytherea," 55 "Wood for
the fireplace," 56 "In a single motion," 57 "Not at
all my favorite author, Kipling described Chicago
once," 58 "Little tendon, tiny as a hair," 59 "Proud
of my half-education now," 60 "Third Class, Queen Mary,
late December on the high Atlantic," 61 "Autumn reminds
me that you bit my lips," 61 "Priests and Freudians
will understand," 62 "Next to my office where I edit
poems," 63 "The Personnel Manager blandly said," 64
"You sat me down and taught me how to edit," 65 "August Saturday night on the Negro street," 66 "I perform in the drug-store window," 66 "One by one my troops
desert," 67 "The Bach *Partitas* saved my life," 68 "Mr.
Cochran flags the train," 69 "Every day when I walk
by the immense publishing company," 70 "In with four
others," 71 "The best book has a bad finality," 72
"There's the green fire of the tropics," 72 "Collect-
ing oneself is like moving to another country," 73
"The molasses of lecturing is sweet," 74 "Always the
character who yells," 74 "I said to Ignotus in the
shadow of the peristyle," 75 "Your book about my

books," 75 "When the last door closes in the wintery
afternoon," 87 "French poetry that always goes itself
one better," 88 "What kind of notation is in my *Time*
file for my life," 89 "As you say (not without sadness)," 90 "Randall, I like your poetry terribly," 91
"They held a celebration for you," 92 "There is prayer
in religion," 93 "The teachers of culture hate science," 94 "To make the child in your own image is a
capital crime," 95 "Each in her well-lighted picture
window," 95 "The prophets say to Know Thyself," 96 "I
drove three thousand miles to ask a question," 97
"The day you discover that your favorite poet is a
homosexual," 98 "Why am I happy writing this textbook,"
99 "They erect a bust of me after my death," 100 "Posterity is a literary racket," 101 "The Jesuit father
said to me," 102 "God couldn't stand the sight of Cain,"
102 "The flesh are exempt for some reason," 103 "What
the analyst said when he came from the exhibit," 104
"The preacher (say Episcopal)," 105 "I'm writing this
poem for someone to see," 106 "In a flash I see my
mistake and put it out of my mind," 107 "Cat called
me a Jewish pig," 108 "He said it: Kill the poet in
yourself," 109 "Dylan wasn't dapper," 110 "As busy
ants tote bales of bread a dozen times their busy
bulk," 111 "Glottal as a bottle, everybody loves you,"
111 "When they ask about your poems I say," 112 "As
richly documented as the hell of priests," 113 "We
pick some unsuspecting soul, usually a friend," 114
"In the Clearing I am at peace," 115 "Balcony Scene,"
116 "Vacation," 116 "Anti-Poem," 117 "Death of a Student," 118 "Basement Apartment," 119 "The Witches Are
Flying," 119 "Teamsters Union," [121] "About the author."

*Notes: When I was teaching for a while in Davis in
1955, I went up to Seattle to give a reading. After-
wards, there was a party and Roethke and all those
people were around. Roethke and I were pretty good
friends. When I walked into the party he was drunk
and shouted out at me, "Well, here comes the bourgeois
poet!" I decided to use that for a title. As far as
the form of the poem goes, the only real precedent I
had for that was a few of the things in* The Place of

Love. *One time I showed that book to St. John Perse
at the Library of Congress. He read it and he said
that I should write in the style of "The Dirty Word";
in other words, the prose poem. That stuck in my mind,
but I didn't do anything about it until this book. By
the way, The Bourgeois Poet was much longer in manuscript. Erskin and I edited the thing down to its present length. I've always felt that I should have re-
edited it, making it less jerky and less obscure.
There is a pretty clear theme. I was going to accept
the fact that I am a bourgeois poet. Instead of doing
the usual thing about taboos of bourgeois values, I
was going to be straight about it. I wanted to say,
"Yeah, I do like living in split-level houses, and so
on." At the same time, I'm of course aware of what's
wrong with that kind of life, but it's the only kind
of life I know. So while the narrative voice in the
book is a persona to a certain extent, the information
there is all true. Like my novel, it's about the paradox of being a poet and a bourgeois American at the
same time. I guess some of my essays, like the one
on Henry Miller, are attempts to throw over that bourgeois side of me, but I can't do it. I could never be
like Bukowski, and I wouldn't want to be. That has
something to do with being a Jew. You go from the
pogroms of Russia to the East Side of New York. Your
father becomes a businessman so you can get an education and become a writer. You don't want to give up
those material things that you just got.*

(b) *First paper edition:*   1964

*Title page, Collation, Pagination, Publication, & Con-
tents as A13a, save measures 8" x 5 1/4".*

Binding: Issued in stiff paper wrappers. Front and
spine, paper blue. Front: [in yellow:] The / Bourgeois
/ Poet / [in white: rule] / [in light blue:] Karl Shapiro / [in white:] $1.95 / (also in cloth, $4.00).
Spine, reading downwards: [in yellow:] The Bourgeois
Poet [in white: rule] [in light blue:] Karl Shapiro
[in white: publisher's emblem] Random House. Back

cover, yellow paper printed in black: [note on K.S.,
photograph by Charles Armstrong, note as front flyleaf of dust jacket of A13a].

A14   RANDALL JARRELL   1967

[in gray:] RANDALL / [in black:] JARRELL / by Karl
Shapiro / [vertical rule] / A lecture presented under
the auspices / of the Gertrude Clarke Whittall Poetry
and / Literature Fund, with a bibliography of / Jarrell materials in the collection of / the Library of
Congress / Published for the Library of Congress by
the / Gertrude Clarke Whittall Poetry and Literature
Fund [device] Washington: 1967

Collation: pp. [i-ii] iii-v [vi] 1-24 [25-26] 27-47
[48-50]; 9" x 5 7/8"; printed on wove paper.

Pagination: p. [1] title page, p. [ii] copyright, p.
iii statement on the Gertrude Clarke Whittall Poetry
and Literature Fund, p. iv acknowledgments, p. v contents, p. [vi] blank, pp. 1-24 text, p. [25] half-
title for bibliography, p. [26] INTRODUCTORY NOTE, KEY
TO SYMBOLS, pp. 27-47 text, pp. [48-50] blank.

Binding: Issued in stiff dark-brown paper wrappers,
stapled. Cover: [in white: drawing of Jarrell] /
RANDALL / JARRELL / by Karl Shapiro. Back: [in white:
Library of Congress emblem]. Inside back cover:
"OTHER PUBLISHED LECTURES PRESENTED UNDER THE AUSPICES
OF THE GERTRUDE CLARKE WHITTALL POETRY AND LITERATURE
FUND."

Publication: Published by the Library of Congress for
the Gertrude Clarke Whittall Poetry and Literature
Fund in 1967 at 25¢. Printed by the U. S. Government
Printing Office.

Contents: 1 "Randall Jarrell," 27 "Bibliography" (compiled by the General Reference and Bibliography Division, Reference Department of the Library of Congress).

A15   THE SOLDIER'S TALE   1968

THE SOLDIER'S TALE

Collation: pp. [1] 2-15; 9" x 5 7/8"; printed on wove
paper.

Pagination: p. [1] title page, pp. 2-15 text.

Binding: Issued in stiff blue paper wrappers, printed
in black and stapled. Front: THE DEPARTMENT / of
MUSIC / [design] / THE SOLDIER'S TALE / (L'Histoire du
Soldat) / Libretto by C. F. Ramuz / as set to music by
/ Igor Stravinsky / adapted and translated / by / Karl
Shapiro / [decorative rule] / The University of Chicago
/ 50¢ April 19 and 20, 1968. Inside front cover: The
University of Chicago gratefully acknowledges the grant
from / the National Translation Center which enabled
the Contemporary / Chamber Players to commission this
translation. / Artistic Director Ralph Shapey / Staged
by James O'Reilly / Choreographed by James Clouser /
Devil Norman Walker / Princess Donna Baldwin / and /
The Contemporary Chamber Players of / The University
of Chicago, conducted / by Ralph Shapey. / [device]
1968 by Karl Shapiro. / All rights reserved. Published 1968; printed in the / United States of America.

Publication: Published by The University of Chicago
Department of Music, April 19, 1968, as a program for
the Contemporary Chamber Players' performance of *The
Soldier's Tale*, at 50¢.

Contents: "The Soldier's Tale" ("L'Histoire du Soldat").

A16   SELECTED POEMS   1968

(a) *First edition:*

Karl Shapiro / Selected Poems / Random House New York

Pagination: pp. [a-b] [i-vi] vii-xiii [xiv] [1-2] 3-
62 [63-64] 65-108 [109-110] 111-113 [114-116] 117-140
[141-142] 143-171 [172-174] 175-185 [186-188] 189-290
[291-292] 293-298 [299-300] 301-333 [334-336]; 8 5/8"
x 6"; printed on wove paper.

Collation: p. [a] blank, p. [b] other books by K.S.,
p. [1] half-title, p. [ii] publisher's emblem, p.
[iii] title page, p. [iv] copyright, acknowledgments,
p. [v] dedication, p. [vi] blank, pp. vii-xiii contents, p. [xiv] blank, p. [1] half-title, p. [2] blank,
pp. 3-62 text, p. [63] half-title, p. [64] blank, pp.
65-108 text, p. [109] half-title, p. [110] blank, pp.
111-113 text, p. [114] blank, p. [115] half-title, p.
[116] blank, pp. 117-140 text, p. [141] half-title, p.
[142] blank, pp. 143-171 text, p. [172] blank, p. [173]
half-title, p. [174] blank, pp. 175-185 text, p. [186]
blank, p. [187] half-title, p. [188] blank, pp. 189-
290 text, p. [291] half-title, p. [292] blank, pp.
293-298 text, p. [299] half-title, p. [300] blank, pp.
301-333 text, p. [334] blank, p. [335] "ABOUT THE
AUTHOR," p. [336] blank.

Binding: Issued in brown cloth covered boards with
black printing. Front cover: KS. Spine, reading downwards: Karl Shapiro [rule] Selected Poems [horizontal:
publisher's emblem] / Random House. White endpapers.

Dust jacket: Issued in dust jacket. Front and spine,
paper gold and brick red. Front: [in brick red:]
Selected / Poems / [in gold:] Karl / Shapiro. Spine,
reading downwards: [in brick red:] Selected Poems [in
gold:] Karl / Shapiro / [horizontal: publisher's em-
blem] / Random / House. Back: [photograph of K. S. by
Ron Warfield] / [in brick red on cream paper:] Karl
Shapiro. Flyleaves, paper in cream, printed in brick
red and black. Front flyleaf lists works from which
selection was made; back flyleaf contains note on K. S.
Designed by Anita Karl.

Publication: Published by Random House, New York,
April 30, 1968, at $7.95. Designed by Betty Anderson.

Contents:

and death in the Garrison State I sing," 195 "Quintana
lay in the shallow grave of coral," 196 "The bourgeois
poet," 197 "Office love," 198 "Lower the standard:
that's my motto," 199 "Waiting in front of the columnar high school," 200 "The dermatologist committed
suicide," 201 "Italy spoiled California for me," 202
"The password of the twentieth century," 203 "It's
lovely," 204 "Abraham Lincoln wore the chimney hat,"
205 "The child who is silent," 206 "One of those idle
autumn evenings," 207 "Libraries," 208 "The two-year-
old has had a motherless week," 209 "All tropic places
smell of mold," 210 "From the top floor of the Tulsa
hotel," 211 "There's a Parthenon in Nashville," 212
"Hart Crane," 213 "Why poetry small and cramped," 214
"Broken bottles hard-set in cement," 215 "The living
rooms of my neighbors," 216 "After the war," 218 "The
History of Philosophy professor," 219 "When suffering
is everywhere, that is the nature of belief," 220 "I
am an atheist who says his prayers," 234 "This Slavic
typist," 235 "In the second-best hotel in Tokyo," 236
"The poet takes the voyage," 237 "Wood for the fireplace," 238 "In a single motion," 239 "Not at all my
favorite author," 240 "Little tendon, tiny as a hair,"
241 "Third Class, *Queen Mary*," 242 "Autumn reminds me,"
243 "Priests and Freudians will understand," 244 "Next
to my office," 245 "August Saturday night," 246 "I
perform in the drug-store window," 247 "One by one my
troops desert," 248 "The Bach *Partitas* saved my life,"
249 "Mr. Cochran flags the train," 250 "Every day when
I walk by," 251 "I said to Ignotus," 252 "Your book
about my books," 253 "French poetry," 255 "What kind
of notation is in my *Time* file," 257 "As you say (not
without sadness), poets don't see, they feel," 258
"Randall, I like your poetry terribly," 259 "They held
a celebration for you," 260 "Each in her well-lighted
picture window," 261 "I drove three thousand miles to
ask a question," 262 "The day you discover," 263 "Why
am I happy writing this textbook," 264 "They erect a
bust of me after my death," 265 "Posterity is a literary racket," 266 "God couldn't stand the sight of
Cain," 267 "The fish are exempt for some reason," 268
"What the analyst said," 269 "The preacher," 270 "I'm
writing this poem for someone to see," 271 "In a flash

I see my mistake," 272 "Cat called me a Jewish pig,"
274 "He said it: Kill the poet in yourself," 275
"Dylan wasn't dapper," 277 "Glottal as a bottle, everybody loves you," 278 "When they ask about your poems,"
279 "As richly documented as the hell of priests," 280
"We pick some unsuspecting soul," 281 "In the Clearing
I am at peace," 282 "Big Sonnet," 293 "Bath-Sheba,"
301 "The Bathers," 303 "New Museum," 305 "Manhole
Covers," 306 "Cadillac," 308 "Western Town," 309 "Party in Winter," 310 "Calling the Child," 311 "A Garden
in Chicago," 312 "Lines for a Unitarian Church," 313
"The House," 314 "The Poetry Reading," 316 "Photographs
of the Poets," 318 "Tornado Warning," 319 "Bad Taste,
Inc.," 320 "Human Nature," 321 "A Drawerful of Eye-
glasses," 322 "Man on Wheels," 323 "You Call These
Poems?" 324 "Emily Dickinson and Katherine Anne Porter," 325 "A Modest Funeral," 326 "Connecticut Valley,"
328 "In India," 330 "California Winter," 332 "Aubade."

(b) *First paper edition:*   1973

Karl Shapiro / Selected Poems / [publisher's emblem]
/ Vintage Books / A Division of Random House [slash]
New York

Pagination, Collation, & Contents as A16a.

Binding: Issued in stiff black paper covers. Front,
in white and black: [inside white rectangle:]
SELECTED / POEMS / [inside white rectangle:] KARL /
SHAPIRO / [inside white rectangle: photograph of K.S.
in gold]. Spine, reading downwards in white and
black: [inside white rectangle:] SELECTED POEMS [in-
side white rectangle:] KARL SHAPIRO / [publisher's
emblem] / V-875 / VINTAGE. Back cover, in white:
POETRY / This edition makes available for the first
/ time in paperback a representative / selection of
poems from the Pulitzer Prize / poet Karl Shapiro.
The volume, containing / over two hundred poems, represents / Shapiro's own choices from *Person, Place /
and Thing, V-Letter and Other Poems, / Essay on Rime,
Trial of a Poet, Poems / 1940-1953, Poems of a Jew*

and / *The Bourgeois Poet.* / 394-71875-5.

Publication: Published by Vintage Books / Random House
in February, 1973, at $2.45.

A17   THERE WAS THAT ROMAN POET WHO FELL IN LOVE AT
FIFTY-ODD   1968

Collation: Broadside; 26" x 23 7/8"; printed in black
on gold wove paper. Max Kahn's two-color woodcut,
16" x 20 1/4", tipped in above poem on folio sheet.

Publication: Included in the portfolio *Ligature 68,*
published by the Madison Park Press, Chicago, in 1968.
Edition size was seventy copies of the portfolio, of
which forty-nine were for sale at $250.00 to museums,
libraries, and public collections, $350.00 to commer-
cial galleries and private collectors. Handset and
printed by John Mitchell of the Acorn Press.

Note: Included in black portfolio. Portfolio itself
was issued in a brown box with black ties; front of
box contains a cream-colored label with brown printing:
LIGATURE / 68. Other poets included are John Frederick Nims, Robert Bly, W. D. Snodgrass, X. J. Kennedy,
Lucian Stryk, Jim Tate, Dave Etter, James Wright, and
Donald Hall. According to the sheet pasted on front
cover of portfolio, "Ligature 68 is a cooperative
portfolio of ten artists and ten poets. It was con-
ceived by a group of artists in 1966 and was finished
in 1968. Seventy copies were made. Twenty artist's
proof copies were distributed to the participating
artists and poets. Of the fifty signed and numbered
copies, forty-nine were made available for purchase.
One copy was presented to Edward Heaine for his help
in handling business and sales. All money received
above costs is shared among the artists."

A18   TO ABOLISH CHILDREN AND OTHER ESSAYS   1968

TO / ABOLISH / CHILDREN [slash] / AND / OTHER / ESSAYS
[slash] / KARL SHAPIRO / CHICAGO [slash] 1968 / QUAD-
RANGLE BOOKS

Collation: pp. [1-13] 14-24 [25] 26-44 [45] 46-62 [63]
64-81 [82] 83-100 [101] 102-131 [132] 133-158 [159]
160-168 [169] 170-288; 8 1/8" x 5 7/8"; printed on
wove paper.

Pagination: p. [1] half-title, p. [2] other books by
K.S., p. [3] title page, p. [4] copyright, p. [5] "To
Teri, who wrote: / *If the bees begin to swarm* / *push
this button to inform* / *the management*," p. [6] blank,
p. [7] contents, p. [8] blank, p. [9] acknowledgments,
p. [10] blank, p. [11] half-title, p. [12] blank, pp.
[13]-288 text.

Binding: Olive green and blue cloth over boards. Cover,
blind-stamped KS. Spine: [decorative rule] / TO / ABOL-
ISH / CHILDREN / & / OTHER / ESSAYS / KARL / SHAPIRO /
[decorative rule] / [publisher's emblem] / QUADRANGLE.
Light blue endpapers.

Dust jacket: Issued in olive green dust jacket. Front
cover: [in green:] To / [in black:] Abolish / Children
/ And Other Essays / [in green:] K [in black:] arl /
Shapiro. Spine: [in green:] To / Abolish / Children
/ Karl / Shapiro / [in black: publisher's emblem] /
Quadrangle. Back cover: [photograph of K.S. by Ron
Warfield] / KARL SHAPIRO. Front flyleaf: [synopsis,
title in green, text in black]. Back flyleaf: [note
on K.S., publisher's emblem and address; title and
emblem in green, text in black]. Designed by Neil
Fujita.

Publication: Published by Quadrangle Books, Inc.,
Chicago, July 5, 1968, at $6.50.

Contents: 13 "To Abolish Children," 25 "The Decolonization of American Literature," 45 "Is Poetry an American Art?" 63 "A Defense of Bad Poetry," 82 "The Image
of the Poet in America," 101 "A Party in Milo," 132
"The Death of Randall Jarrell," 159 "To Revive Anarch-
ism," 169 "A *Maleboolge* of Fourteen Hundred Books."

Karl Shapiro
Selected Poems

Random House   New York

EDSEL

by

Karl Shapiro

Published by

BERNARD GEIS ASSOCIATES

A20

THE POETRY WRECK
Selected Essays: 1950-1970
KARL SHAPIRO

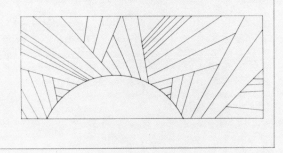

A22

ADULT BOOKSTORE

Karl Shapiro

Random House
New York

A23

A19 WHITE-HAIRED LOVER   1968

KARL SHAPIRO / WHITE-HAIRED / LOVER / RANDOM HOUSE
NEW YORK

Collation: pp. [i-x] [1-2] 3-37 [38]; 8 1/2" x 5 3/4";
printed on laid paper.

Pagination: [1] blank, p. [ii] KARL SHAPIRO, p. [iii]
half-title, p. [iv] blank, p. [v] title page, p. [vi]
copyright, acknowledgments, p. [vii] "for TERI / *My
glass shall not persuade me I am old*," p. [viii] blank,
p. [ix] contents, p. [x] blank, p. [1] half-title, p.
[2] blank, pp. 3-37 text, p. [38] ABOUT THE AUTHOR.

Binding: Covers: gray paper over boards. Spine: gray
cloth over boards. Front cover: decorative KS blind-
stamped. Spine, reading downwards: [in white:] KARL
SHAPIRO WHITE-HAIRED LOVER RANDOM HOUSE. Decorative
endpapers, white with black printing.

Dust jacket: Issued in cream-colored dust jacket.
Front cover: [in gray:] White- / -Haired / Lover /
[decorative rule] / [in red:] Karl / Shapiro / [in
gray:] A RANDOM HOUSE BOOK. Spine, reading downwards:
[in gray:] White-Haired Lover [rule] [in red:] Karl
Shapiro [in gray:] RANDOM HOUSE. Back cover: [photo-
graph of K.S. by Ron Warfield]. Front flyleaf: "A
celebratory cycle of twenty-nine love / poems. In
these new poems, highly personal / and frankly erotic,
Karl Shapiro returns / to the traditional verse form
that he / temporarily abandoned in *The Bourgeois /
Poet* (1964). Only one of these poems has / previously
appeared in book form / (in *Selected Poems*, 1968).
/ JACKET DESIGN: ANITA KARL." Back flyleaf: [note on
K.S.].

Publication: Published by Random House, September 19,
1968, at $4.00. Printed and bound by the Book Press,
Inc., Brattleboro, Vermont. Typeset by the Typo-
graphic Service Company, New York. Designed by
Richard-Gabriel Rummonds.

Contents: 3 "There Was That Roman Poet," 4 "You Played
Chopin," 5 "I Swore to Stab the Sonnet," 6 "How Beau-
tifully You Clothe Your Body," 7 "He Loves the Chase,"
8 "The Dark Exciting Days," 9 "There Is Gray in My
Eyebrows," 10 "How Do I Love You?" 11 "Love, It Is
Time," 12 "I Do Not Want to Recognize Your Face," 13
"If I Should Die," 14 "Roses, Poetry," 15 "You Lay
Above Me," 16 "O My Beloved," 17 "I Am the Clown," 18
"It's Morning," 19 "How Do You Walk?" 21 "In St. Louis
in a Hundred and Four Degrees," 22 "It's Getting Ready
to Storm," 23 "The Sad Thing Is," 24 "Aubade," 27 "Bal-
lade," 29 "Now Christ Is Risen," 30 "Words for a Wall-
Painting," 31 "After the Storm," 32 "You, Lying with
Your Back to Me," 33 "Reeking with Love," 34 "July the
Fourth," 35 "Epithalamium, the Second Time Around."

A20   EDSEL   1971

(a) *First edition:*

EDSEL / by / Karl Shapiro / [device] / *Published by* /
BERNARD GEIS ASSOCIATES

Collation: pp. [i-iv] [1-2] 3-308; 8 1/2" x 5 1/2";
printed on wove paper.

Pagination: p. [i] half-title, p. [ii] *By Karl Shapiro*,
p. [iii] title page, p. [iv] copyright, p. [1] dedication, p. [2] "Among the Just / Be just, among the
Filthy, filthy too. / Auden," pp. 3-308 text.

Binding: Front and back cover, gold paper over boards.
Spine, burgundy cloth over boards, stamped in silver:
KARL / SHAPIRO / [vertical:] EDSEL / [horizontal:]
BERNARD GEIS / ASSOCIATES / [publisher's emblem].
White endpapers.

Dust jacket: Issued in dust jacket with gold, yellow,
and pink bands. Front cover: EDSEL / Karl Shapiro /
the poet's first novel. Spine: [in black:] Karl /
Shapiro [slash] [in red:] Edsel / [in black:] BERNARD

GEIS / ASSOCIATES / [publisher's emblem]. Flyleaves, paper in yellow, text in black, titles in red. Front flyleaf: [synopsis of book]. Back flyleaf: [synopsis of book continued] / [photograph of K.S.] / [note on K.S.]. Designed by The Design Room.

Publication: Publication by Bernard Geis Associates, New York, May 28, 1971, at $6.95.

Contents: Edsel.

Note: Edsel *is autobiographical in the sense that it has to do with my uneasiness at being in the academy --the pretense of being a professor when you're not, having to live one kind of life on campus, and a secret, degenerate life when you're off. I had trouble getting the book published. Random House didn't want it and New Directions thought I was just trying to make money. Somebody mentioned to me that I should send it to Bernard Geis. I'd never heard of him, but I did it. He called me up after reading a couple chapters and said he wanted to do the book. I was supposed to get half of the fifty thousand dollar check for paperback rights, but Geis went bankrupt and kept the whole thing. That happened to all his writers. I really didn't care that much about the money, but the whole thing more or less forced the book out of print. Edsel is now a rare book.*

I'm thinking about doing another novel, not like Edsel *but using the same theme--the poet in a middle-class world. I can write fiction very fast, sometimes a chapter a day. I wrote much of* Edsel *on a beach in Tampa when Teri and I were on vacation. There were some friends of ours from Chicago there, and everytime I'd finish a page, he'd come tearing across the sand to grab it and read it hot off the typewriter. I first started writing the book in the style of Sam Beckett's* How It Is, *that telegraphic style, and the hero's name was Botts. But that didn't work out.*

(b) *First paper edition:*   1972

EDSEL / [rule] / *By Karl Shapiro* / [publisher's em-
blem] / A SIGNET BOOK from / NEW AMERICAN LIBRARY /
[rule] TIMES MIRROR

Collation: pp. [1-6] 7-288; 7" x 4 1/8"; printed on
wove paper.

Pagination: p. [1] *"EDSEL / IS THE NOVEL THAT / AN-
SWERS THE QUESTION:* / Can a world-famous poet survive
in the / whacky wonderland of a mid-western / university where sex and verse are / free, honesty and
integrity costly, / every conceivable fashionable
hang- / up is assiduously cultivated, and all / things
conspire to destroy him both / as a poet and a man? /
*Karl Shapiro is one of America's leading / poets.
With* Edsel, *he has taken a bold / new step in modern
fiction.* / [blurb from review of A20a]," p. [2] ad
for other Signet Books, p. [3] title page, p. [4]
copyright, p. [5] dedication, p. [6] blank, pp. 7-288
text.

Binding: Issued in stiff paper covers; front and back
covers: photograph of lovers. Front cover: [in black:
publisher's emblem] A SIGNET NOVEL [device] Y5123
[device] $1.25 / [in white:] A PULITZER PRIZE-WINNER
/ WRITES A STEAMING, IRREVERENT / SEXUAL-LITERARY
FIRST NOVEL. / "... THE FUNNIEST, RAUNCHIEST, MOST /
DELICIOUS AND PROVOCATIVE / NOVEL OF THE YEAR!" /
--Chicago News / EDSEL / [rule] KARL / SHAPIRO.
Spine: [in white: publisher's emblem] / SIGNET / Y /
[in gold:] 5123 / [reading downwards, in white:]
EDSEL KARL SHAPIRO 451-Y5123-125. Back cover: [in
white:] MEET EDSEL LAZEROW ... / Poet on the loose
in an up-tight university. / Savant on the sly to the
freaked-out / student body. Male on the make among
the / restless campus wives, rebellious co-eds, /
and lovely lewd ladies of the town. / Put it all together and you have the / unforgettable hero of the
wildest, wittiest, / most outrageous and devastating
novel / of the year. / [blurbs from reviews of A20a]
/ NEW AMERICAN LIBRARY PUBLISHES SIGNET, SIGNETTE,
MENTOR, CLASSIC, PLUME & NAL BOOKS.

Publication: Published by the New American Library in August, 1972, at $1.25.

Contents: As A20a.

A21   AUDEN (1907-1973)   1974

AUDEN / (1907-1973) / a new poem by Karl Shapiro

Collation: pp. [1-4]; 10" x 7 1/4"; printed on wove paper.

Pagination: p. [1] title page, p. [2] woodcut of K.S. by Diana Friedman, p. [3] text, p. [4] statement of limitation, signatures of poet and artist, copyright.

Binding: Issued in dark brown paper wrappers. Front wrapper: AUDEN [device] (1907-1973) / a new poem by Karl Shapiro. Back wrapper: Number 1 in a series sponsored by the / Library Associates, UCD. Sewn with tie outside.

Publication: Published by the Library Associates, University of California, Davis, in November, 1974, at $4.25. 175 copies, numbered and signed by K.S. and Diana Friedman. Printed by Sid Berger, assisted by L.A.B., C.S.B., D.P., and M.L.W. Handset and printed on Columbian Press.

Contents: "Auden (1907-1973)."

A22   THE POETRY WRECK   1975

THE POETRY WRECK / Selected Essays: 1950-1970 / KARL SHAPIRO / [design]

Collation: pp. [i-xii] xiii [xiv] xv-xvii [xviii] [1-2] 3-365 [366]; 8 5/8" x 5 7/8"; printed on wove paper.

Pagination: p. [1] blank, p. [ii] other books by K.S.,
p. [iii] half-title, p. [iv] *RANDOM HOUSE* [publisher's
emblem] *NEW YORK*, p. [v] title page, p. [vi] copyright,
acknowledgments, pp. [vii-ix] acknowledgments continued,
p. [x] blank, p. [xi] dedication, p. [xii] blank, p.
xiii contents, p. [xiv] blank, pp. xv-xvii foreword,
p. [xviii] blank, p. [1] half-title, p. [2] blank, pp.
3-365 text, p. [366] About the Author.

Binding: Front and back covers, light brown paper over
boards; spine, dark brown cloth over boards. Printed
in gold. Front cover: KS [inset design]. Spine: *THE
/ POETRY / WRECK / KARL / SHAPIRO* [inside decorative
rules] *Selected / Essays / 1950-1970 /* [publisher's
emblem] / *Random House.* White endpapers.

Dust jacket: Issued in white dust jacket. Front cover,
inside brown rules: [in black:] THE [design] / POETRY
/ WRECK / [in brown:] SELECTED ESSAYS / 1950-1970 /
KARL / SHAPIRO. Spine, inside blue rules, reading
downwards in two lines: [in black:] THE POETRY WRECK /
[in brown:] KARL SHAPIRO [in blue: publisher's emblem]
RANDOM HOUSE. Back cover: [blurbs from reviews of
books by K.S.] Front flyleaf: $10.00 / [synopsis].
Back flyleaf: [photograph of K.S. by Lisa Baldwin] /
[note on K.S.] / Jacket design: Muriel Nasser / [pub-
lisher's address] / 3 [slash] 75.

Publication: Published by Random House, New York,
February 11, 1975, at $10.00.

Contents: xv Foreword, 3 "T.S. Eliot: The Death of
Literary Judgement," 29 "Ezra Pound: The Scapegoat of
Modern Poetry," 55 "W. B. Yeats: Trial by Culture,"
83 "The Retreat of W. H. Auden," 111 "William Carlos
Williams: The True Contemporary," 139 "Dylan Thomas,"
156 "The First White Aboriginal," 175 "The Greatest
Living Patagonian," 201 "The Decolonization of American Literature," 224 "Is Poetry an American Art?"
245 "The True Artificer," 268 "The Death of Randall
Jarrell," 300 "The Career of the Poem," 323 "American Poet?" 353 "The Poetry Wreck."

ADULT / BOOKSTORE / [rule] / Karl Shapiro / [publish-
er's emblem] / Random House / New York

Collation: pp. [i-viii] ix-x [1-2] 3-32 [33-34] 35-53
[54-56] 57-79 [80-86]; 8 1/2" x 5 3/4"; printed on
wove paper.

Pagination: p. [1] blank, p. [ii] other books by K.S.,
p. [iii] half-title, p. [iv] blank, p. [v] title page,
p. [vi] copyright, acknowledgments, p. [vii] dedication,
p. [viii] blank, pp. ix-x contents, p. [1] half-title,
p. [2] blank, pp. 3-32 text, p. [33] FROM CALIFORNIA,
p. [34] blank, pp. 35-53 text, p. [54] blank, p. [55]
OVER MANY SEAS, p. [56] blank, pp. 57-79 text, p. [80]
blank, p. [81] note on K.S., pp. [82-86] blank.

Binding: Front and back covers, white decorative paper
over boards. Spine: burgundy cloth over boards. Front
cover: [in gold, lower right-hand corner:] K / [rule]
/ S. Spine, reading downwards: [in silver:] ADULT
BOOKSTORE [rule] Karl Shapiro [rule] Random House.
White endpapers.

Dust jacket: Issued in purple dust jacket. Front:
[in gray, rules; in white:] ADULT / BOOKSTORE / [in
orange:] POEMS BY KARL / SHAPIRO. Spine, reading
downwards: [in white:] ADULT BOOKSTORE [in orange:]
KARL SHAPIRO [in gray: publisher's emblem] [in white:]
RANDOM HOUSE. Back: [photograph of K.S. by Teri
Shapiro] / [note on K.S.; title in orange, text in
white]. Flyleaves: white paper, text in black inside
purple rules. Front flyleaf: [synopsis]. Back flyleaf: [list of Random House books by K.S., with
KARL SHAPIRO in purple] / Jacket design: Muriel Nasser
/ [publisher's address] / 4 [slash] 76.

Publication: Published by Random House, New York, in
1976 at $6.00.

Contents: 3 "A Parliament of Poets," 5 "The Humanities

Building," 7 "Flying First Class," 9 "Adult Bookstore,"
11 "Girls Working in Banks," 13 "Crossing Lincoln Park,"
15 "The White Negress," 16 "Jefferson's Greeting," 17
"My Father's Funeral," 20 "The Sense of Beauty," 23
"Writer in Exile," 25 "The Heiligenstadt Testament,"
35 "Moving in," 37 "Moon-Walk," 38 "The Moss Roses,"
40 "A Curiosity," 41 "Detail," 42 "Garage Sale," 44
"The Martini," 45 "California Petrarchan," 46 "Death
of the Fig," 48 "The Piano Tuner's Wife," 49 "Mature
Garden," 50 "The Garage Fool," 51 "My Fame's Not Feeling Well," 52 "Sestina: of the Militant Vocabulary,"
57 "The Stroke and the Dot," 58 "Eclogue: America and
Japan," 66 "Death of the *Yamoto*," 70 "Over Many Seas,"
71 "To Lesbia," 72 "The Rape of Philomel."

Note: I wrote all the poems in Adult Bookstore *in
Davis, California, with the exception of the Japanese
poem, the dramatic monologue. That is a re-write from
an unpublished one-act play I did about the American
re-location camps for the Japanese. Actually, it was
published in Japanese, but not in English. I wanted
"Adult Bookstore" to be the title poem because I once
made a movie of that title and it was never distributed
--the distributor said that it was too hot to handle,
the schools wouldn't buy it. Well, we had worked a
long time on that film, and I thought "Adult Bookstore"
was my kind of poem.*

B. BOOKS COAUTHORED, EDITED, INTRODUCED

B1   FIVE YOUNG AMERICAN POETS   1941

[in black decorative borders:] FIVE YOUNG / AMERICAN
/ POETS / Second Series 1941 / Paul Goodman [device]
Jeanne McGahey / Clark Mills [device] David Schubert
/ Karl Shapiro / [outside border:] NEW DIRECTIONS
[publisher's emblem] NORFOLK, CONN.

Collation: pp. [i–vi] [1–3] 4–44 [45–47] 48–88 [89–91]
92–132 [133–135] 136–172 [173–218]; 8 1/2" x 5 1/2";
printed on wove paper.

Pagination: p. [i] half-title, p. [ii] blank, p. [iii]
title page, p. [iv] copyright, *"The* Five Young American Poets *anthology will be / published annually and
poets under thirty who have / not published a book of
verse are invited to compete / for a place in it. Anyone wishing to submit a manu- / script is asked, however, to write first to the Editor of / New Directions
at Norfolk, Conn., enclosing a stamped, / addressed
envelope, so that we may send shipping instructions,"*
p. [v] contents, p. [vi] blank, p. [1] Cain and Abel /
Paul Goodman, p. [2] note on Paul Goodman, p. [3] holograph of Goodman poem, pp. 4–44 text, p. [45] The
White Box / *Jeanne McGahey,* p. [46] note on Jeanne
McGahey, p. [47] holograph of McGahey poem, pp. 48–88
text, p. [89] Speech / After Darkness / *Clark Mills,*
p. [90] note on Clark Mills, p. [91] holograph of
Mills poem, pp. 92–132 text, p. [133] The Simple Scale
/ *for Judy and for Peak / David Schubert,* p. [134]
note on David Schubert, p. [135] holograph of Schubert
poem, pp. 136–172 text, p. [173] Noun / *Karl Shapiro,*
p. [174] note on K.S., p. [175] holograph of K.S. poem,
pp. 176–218 text.

Binding: Green cloth over boards. Spine stamped in
gold: [in borders:] FIVE / YOUNG / AMERICAN / POETS
/ [rule] / NEW / DIRECTIONS / [outside borders:]
SECOND / GROUP / 1941. White endpapers.

Dust jacket: Issued in dust jacket [unexamined].

Publication: Published by James Laughlin, New Direc-

tions, in 1941. Printed by the American Book-Strat-
ford Press, Inc., New York.

Contents: Shapiro's contributions include 176-177 "A
Note on Poetry," 178-179 "The Dome of Sunday," 180-181
"Alexandria," 182 "Emporium," 183-184 "The Confirmation," 185-188 "Druid Hill Park," 189 "Mongolian Idiot,"
190 "Drug Store," 191-193 "Elegy Written on a Frontporch," 194-195 "Midnight Show," 196-197 "Hospital,"
198-199 "Honkytonk," 200 "Necropolis," 201-202 "Death
of Emma Goldman," 203-204 "Auto Wreck," 205-206 "Hollywood," 207 "Israfel," 208-209 "Washington Cathedral,"
210-211 "University," 212-213 "Buick," 214-215 "Scyros,"
216-218 "Conscription Camp."

B2   POETS AT WORK   1948

Poets at Work / ESSAYS BASED ON THE MODERN POETRY /
COLLECTION AT THE LOCKWOOD MEMORIAL / LIBRARY, UNI-
VERSITY OF BUFFALO, *by* RUDOLF ARNHEIM / W. H. AUDEN /
KARL SHAPIRO / DONALD A. STAUFFER / *Introduction by*
CHARLES D. ABBOTT / *New York* / HARCOURT, BRACE AND
COMPANY

Collation: pp. [i-vi] vii-ix [x] [1-2] 3-36 [37-38]
39-82 [83-84] 85-121 [122-124] 125-162 [163-164] 165-
181 [182] 183-186; 8" x 5 1/4"; printed on wove paper.

Pagination: p. [i] half-title, p. [ii] blank, p. [iii]
title page, p. [iv] copyright, statement of first
edition, p. [v] contents, p. [vi] list of illustrations, pp. vii-ix foreword, p. [x] acknowledgment, p.
[1] text, p. [2] illustration, pp. 3-36 text, p. [37]
half-title, p. [38] illustration, pp. 39-82 text, p.
[83] half-title, p. [84] illustration, pp. 85-121 text,
p. [122] blank, p. [123] half-title, p. [124] illustration, pp. 125-162 text, p. [163] text, p. [164]
illustration, pp. 165-181 text, p. [182] blank, pp.
183-186 index.

Binding: Issued in dark red cloth over boards. Stamped

in gold on spine: ARNHEIM / AUDEN / SHAPIRO / STAUFFER / [in black rectangle:] *Poets* / *at* / *Work* / [below rectangle:] Harcourt, Brace / and Company. White endpapers.

Dust jacket: Issued in dust jacket [unexamined].

Publication: Published by Harcourt, Brace and Company in 1948.

Contents: Shapiro's contribution is [83]-121 "The Meaning of the Discarded Poem."

B3 MODERN AMERICAN & MODERN BRITISH POETRY   1955

MODERN AMERICAN / & / MODERN BRITISH / *Poetry* / REVISED, SHORTER EDITION / *Edited by Louis Untermeyer* / IN CONSULTATION WITH / KARL SHAPIRO AND RICHARD WILBUR / HARCOURT, BRACE & WORLD, INC. / NEW YORK CHICAGO SAN FRANCISCO ATLANTA

Collation: pp. [i-ix] x-xxx [xxxi] xxxii [1-3] 4-685 [686-687] 688-697 [698-704]; 7 7/8" x 4 5/8"; printed on wove paper.

Pagination: p. [i] half-title, p. [ii] blank, p. [iii] title page, pp. [iv-vii] copyright, acknowledgments, p. [viii] blank, pp. [ix]-xxx contents, pp. [xxxi]-xxxii foreword, p. [1] half-title, p. [2] blank, pp. [3]-685 text, p. [686] blank, pp. [687]-697 index, pp. [698-704] blank.

Binding: Issued in pale blue cloth over boards, with title on front cover and spine on purple cloth. Front cover, in white: MODERN / AMERICAN / & MODERN / BRITISH / *Poetry*. Spine, in white: *UNTERMEYER* / *with* / *Shapiro & Wilbur* / MODERN / AMERICAN / & MODERN / BRITISH / *Poetry* / REVISED / SHORTER EDITION / HARCOURT, BRACE / & WORLD. White endpapers.

Dust jacket: Issued without dust jacket.

Publication: Published by Harcourt, Brace & World, New York, April 8, 1955.

Contents: This is a revised edition of Louis Untermeyer's *Mid-Century Edition*, published in 1950. K.S. collaborated on the editing of this volume. In addition, his poems include "The Leg," "The Dome of Sunday," "October 1," "Poet," "Buick," "Necropolis," "The Progress of Faust," "The Sickness of Adam," "The Recognition of Eve."

B4   THE TENOR   1957

(a) *First edition:*

HUGO WEISGALL / *the* / *Tenor* / [rule] / OPERA in *One Act* / *(Based on* DER KAMMERSANGER *by Frank Wedekind) / libretto by* KARL SHAPIRO *and* ERNST LERT / MERION MUSIC, INC. / THEODORE PRESSER CO., Sole Agent / Bryn Mawr, Pennsylvania / [device] Copyright 1956 (Mss.) by Merion Music Inc., /International Copyright Secured / All Rights Reserved / Printed in U.S.A.

Collation: pp. [i-vi] 1-153 [154]; 12" x 9"; printed on wove paper.

Pagination: pp. [i-ii] blank, p. [iii] title page, p. [iv] note, p. [v] characters and synopsis, p. [vi] synopsis continued, instrumentation, duration, pp. 1-153 text, p. [154] blank.

Binding: Issued in light tan covers. Front cover: [in black:] HUGO WEISGALL / [in blue:] *the* / *Tenor* / [rule] / [in black:] OPERA *in One Act* / MERION MUSIC, INC. / Theodore Presser Co., sole agent / Bryn Mawr, Pennsylvania / $5.00. Spine, reading downwards: THE TENOR--*Hugo Weisgall*.

Publication: Published by Merion Music, Inc., October 29, 1957, at $5.00.

Contents: "The Tenor."

Note: The world premiere of *The Tenor* was held February 11, 1952. K.S. collaborated on the libretto with Ernst Lert, at least as credited on the title page. According to K.S.: *I did all the work myself. Ernst Lert barely knew English. The one contribution Lert made was to ask me to write a scene with a manager. He was a difficult man to work with--he found fault with everyone, including the composer and me.*

(b) *Record edition:*   1957

THE TENOR / Opera in One Act / (Based on *Der Kammersanger* by Frank Wedekind) / *Music by* / Hugo Weisgall / *Libretto by* / Karl Shapiro and Ernst Lert / Merion Music, Inc. / Theodore Presser Co., Sole Agent / [device] / Copyright 1956 (Mss.) by Merion Music, Inc. / Published 1957 by Merion Music, Inc. / International Copyright Secured / All Rights Reserved / Printed in U.S.A.

Collation: pp. [1-3] 4-30 [31-32]; 9 1/2" x 6 3/4"; printed on wove paper.

Pagination: p. [1] title page, p. [2] note, list of characters, synopsis, p. [3] synopsis continued, pp. 4-30 text, pp. [31-32] blank.

Binding: Issued in light blue wrappers, stapled. Front cover: [decorative rule, publisher's emblem, decorative rule] / HUGO WEISGALL / [rule] / THE TENOR / [rule] / Opera in One Act / (Based on *Der Kammersanger* by Frank Wedekind) / *Libretto by* / Karl Shapiro and Ernst Lert / [photograph].

Publication: Published by Merion Music, Inc., October 29, 1957. Included with recording of *The Tenor* released by Westminster.

B5 AMERICAN POETRY   1960

(a) *First edition:*

AMERICAN POETRY / [device] *Edited by Karl Shapiro /
Thomas Y. Crowell Company* / [device] New York [device]
Established 1834

Collation: pp. [i-iv] v-viii [ix] x-xvii [xviii-xx]
1-259 [260] 261-265 [266-268];   9 1/2" x 6 1/4";
printed on wove paper.

Pagination: p. [i] half-title, p. [ii] *Reader's Bookshelf of American Literature*, p. [iii] title page, p.
[iv] copyright, acknowledgments, pp. v-viii acknowledgments continued, pp. [ix]-xvii contents, p. [xviii]
blank, p. [xix] half-title, p. [xx] blank, pp. 1-8
"What Is American Poetry?" pp. 9-239 text, pp. 240-243
"On Poetry and Poets," pp. 244-256 notes, pp. 257-259
"Suggested Critical Readings," p. [260] blank, pp.
261-265 Index, pp. [266-268] blank.

Binding: Light yellowish green cloth covered boards.
Spine: [in black:] American / Poetry / [decorative
band, blue with two rules and eagle stamped in gold]
/ [in black:] *Shapiro / Crowell.* White endpapers.

Dust jacket: Issued in light blue dust jacket. Front
cover: [in black: drawing of eagle] / [in white:]
American / Poetry / [in black:] Edited by *Karl Shapiro*
/ [black and white photograph] / [in white:] *Reader's
Bookshelf of American Literature.* Spine: [in white:]
American / Poetry / [white band with line drawing of
eagle in black] / [black band, in blue:] *Shapiro* /
[blue band, in black:] *Crowell.* Back cover: [pub-
lisher's device]. Flyleaves, white paper with black
printing; text lists contents and notes. Front cover
photograph by Ansel Adams, back cover device by Oscar
Ogg from *The 26 Letters.* Designed by Laurel Wagner.

Publication: Published by Thomas Y. Crowell Company,
March 2, 1960, at $5.95. Printed by Vail-Ballou Press,
Inc., Binghamton, New York.

Contents: K.S. edited this anthology. His own selections include the prose pieces 1 "What Is American
Poetry," 240 "On Poetry and Poets," 244 "Notes on
Poets," and 257 "Suggested Critical Readings." Also
included is his poem 217 "Adam and Eve."

(b) *First paper edition:*   1960

American Poetry / [device] Edited by *Karl Shapiro* /
UNIVERSITY OF NEBRASKA / *Thomas Y. Crowell Company*
[device] New York [device] Established 1834

Collation, Pagination, & Contents as B5a, save measures 9 1/2" x 6".

Binding: Issued in blue paper covers. Front cover:
[in black: drawing of eagle] / [in white:] American
Poetry / [in black:] *Edited by Karl Shapiro* / [in
white:] AMERICAN LITERARY FORMS. Spine, reading downwards: [in white] American Poetry [in black:] *Shapiro*
/ [in white:] *Crowell*. Back cover: list of books and
editors in the series, quotation from foreword, and
artist's credit in white.

Publication: Published by Thomas Y. Crowell Company,
March 2, 1960, at $2.75.

Note: This is the first appearance of Allen Ginsberg's
Howl in an anthology of major American poetry. *I was
aware of what was going on in San Francisco, and I
admired people like Ferlinghetti and Rexroth. I
thought Ginsberg's poem was a real breakthrough. At
the same time, you've got to remember that I've always been very much against censorship. I was in San
Francisco when* Howl *was getting ready to go on trial,
and I offered my services to Ginsberg. It turned out
I was in Japan when the whole thing started. When William Van O'Connor got a contract to do his big series of
anthologies in American Literature, he asked me to do the
poetry. I told him that I'd like to do it, but that I'd
like to make it from Anne Bradstreet to Allen Ginsberg;
I wanted them to print the unexpurgated version of*
Howl. *Bill said it was fine with him, and it was fine*

60

with the publisher, but there was one incident with a
woman who worked in the office. She really freaked
out about including Howl; she started writing people
all over the country, making long-distance phone calls.
It was a terrible thing. The mess finally got to the
point where Thomas Crowell himself called me up to
apologize. I thought Howl was very representative of
American poetry at the time, a wonderful climax to the
book.

B6 THE YEAR OF THE GREEN WAVE   1960

(a) *First edition:*

BRUCE CUTLER / The Year of the Green Wave / [illustra-
tion] / UNIVERSITY OF NEBRASKA PRESS / LINCOLN [de-
vice] 1960

Collation: pp. [i-iv] v-vii [viii-x] xi-xii [xiii-xiv]
[1-4] 5-17 [18-20] 21-46 [47-48] 49-52 [53-54] 55-64
[65-66]; 8" x 5 1/4"; printed on wove paper.

Pagination: p. [i] half-title, p. [ii] blank, p. [iii]
title page, p. [iv] acknowledgments, copyright, pp.
v-vii introduction, p. [viii] blank, p. [ix] dedication, p. [x] blank, pp. xi-xii contents, p. [xiii]
half-title, p. [xiv] blank, p. [1] text, p. [2] blank,
p. [3] section number, p. [4] blank, pp. 5-17 text, p.
[18] blank, p. [19] section number, p. [20] blank, pp.
21-46 text, p. [47] section number, p. [48] blank, pp.
49-52 text, p. [53] section number, p. [54] blank, pp.
55-64 text, p. [65] note on series, p. [66] blank.

Binding: Issued in pale green paper-covered boards,
with a black cloth backstrip. Spine, reading downwards, in gold: CUTLER THE YEAR OF THE GREEN WAVE
NEBRASKA. White endpapers.

Dust jacket: Issued in white dust jacket. Front:
bruce cutler / the year of / the / green / wave /
foreword by / karl shapiro. Spine, reading downwards:

cutler the year of the green wave nebraska. Decoration in green and black on bottom of front cover, spine, and back cover.

Publication: Published by the University of Nebraska Press, April 25, 1960, at $3.00. This was the first book in the University of Nebraska's First-Book Poetry Series. According to the note at the end of the book, "As its name indicates, the First-Book Poetry Series is devoted to the work of contemporary poets whose poems have not previously been collected. One or more collections a year are nominated for publication in the series by an editorial board consisting of KARL SHAPIRO, BERNICE SLOTE, and JAMES E. MILLER, JR. In making their selections the editors look particularly for emphasis on the American feeling for life as shown in writers like Whitman, Emerson, Mark Twain, Hart Crane, and William Carlos Williams."

Contents: v "Introduction [by K.S.]."

(b) *First paper edition:*   1960

Title page, Collation, Pagination, & Contents as B6a. Issued in stiff paper wrappers, printed as dust jacket of B6a. Published at $2.00.

B7   START WITH THE SUN   1960

(a) *First edition:*

By JAMES E. MILLER, JR. / KARL SHAPIRO, *and* / BERNICE SLOTE / START / WITH / THE / SUN / *Studies in Cosmic Poetry*

Collation: pp. [i-iv] v-viii [1-2] 3-11 [12-14] 15-53 [54-56] 57-134 [135-136] 137-165 [166-168] 169-190 [191-192] 193-225 [226-228] 229-238 [239-240] 241-249 [250] 251-257 [258] 259-260 [261-264]; 9" x 6"; printed on wove paper.

Pagination: p. [i] half-title, p. [ii] UNIVERSITY OF
NEBRASKA PRESS / *Lincoln, 1960* / [illustration of sun
in yellow, crosses over into p. iii] / [in sun:] What
we want to ... re-establish / the living organic con-
nections / with the cosmos, the sun and earth, / with
mankind and nation and family. / Start with the sun,
and the rest / will slowly, slowly happen. / D.H.
LAWRENCE / *Apocalypse*, p. [iii] title page, p. [iv]
copyright, acknowledgments, pp. v-vi foreword, pp. vii-
viii contents, p. [1] *The* WHITMAN TRADITION, p. [2]
blank, pp. 3-11 text, p. [12] blank, p. [13] *Part I* /
THE ELEMENTS / [from Whitman's *Leaves of Grass*, 3
lines], p. [14] blank, pp. 15-53 text, p. [54] blank,
p. [55] *Part II* / WHITMAN *and* LAWRENCE / [from Lawrence's *Apocalypse*, 3 lines] p. [56] blank, pp. 57-
134 text, p. [135] *Part III* / WHITMAN *and* CRANE /
[from Hart Crane's *The Bridge*, 4 lines], p. [136]
blank, pp. 137-165 text, p. [166] blank, p. [167] *Part
IV* / WHITMAN *and* THOMAS / [from Dylan Thomas' *Fern Hill*,
2 lines], p. [168] blank, pp. 169-190 text, p. [191]
Part V / EXTENSIONS / [from Whitman's *Poets to Come,*
2 lines], p. [192] blank, pp. 193-225 text, p. [226]
blank, p. [227] START WITH THE SUN, p. [228] blank, pp.
229-238 text, p. [239] NOTES AND / BIBLIOGRAPHY, p.
[240] blank, pp. 241-249 text, p. [250] blank, pp. 251-
257 index, p. [258] blank, pp. 259-260 acknowledgments,
pp. [261-264] blank.

Binding: Issued in blue cloth over boards. Stamped in
gold on front cover: START WITH THE SUN / *Studies in
Cosmic Poetry*. Stamped in gold on spine: MILLER /
SHAPIRO / SLOTE / START / WITH / THE / SUN / [device]
/ NEBRASKA. Yellow endpapers.

Dust jacket: Issued in dust jacket [unexamined].

Publication: Published by the University of Nebraska
Press, June 20, 1960, at $4.75.

Contents: Contributions by K.S. include 29 "Cosmic
Consciousness," 57 "The First White Aboriginal," 193
"The Greatest Living Patagonian," 206 "The True Con-
temporary."

Note: "Cosmic Consciousness," "The Greatest Living Patagonian," and "The True Contemporary" were based on lectures given by K.S. under the Elliston Foundation at the University of Chicago.

(b) *First paper edition:*   1963

Title page, Collation, Pagination, & Contents as B7a, save on title page *Studies in the Whitman Tradition* replaces *Studies in Cosmic Poetry*, illustration of yellow sun is deleted, and p. [261] contains a note on the authors. Book measures 8" x 5 1/4".

Binding: Issued in yellow paper wrappers, with decorative red and white specks. Front: [illustration of the sun] / START WITH / THE SUN / STUDIES IN THE WHIT-MAN TRADITION / JAMES E. MILLER, JR. / KARL SHAPIRO / BERNICE SLOTE / [publisher's emblem] $1.50. Spine: [publisher's emblem] / [device] MILLER [device] SHA-PIRO [device] / [device] SLOTE [device] / START WITH THE SUN / BB 165. Back cover: [white background, black printing:] *Winner of the 1960 Poetry Chap-Book / Award of the Poetry Society of America* / [quotation from M. Cowley, 10 lines] / [list of contents, 20 lines] / *Cover design by Jack Brodie.*

Publication: Published by the University of Nebraska Press as a Bison Book in March, 1963, at $1.50.

B8   A CORRESPONDENCE OF AMERICANS   1960

[in script:] Jack Hirschman / [device] a / correspondence / of Americans / [vertical rule] / INDIANA UNI-VERSITY PRESS / 1960 [device] BLOOMINGTON

Collation: pp. [1-12] 15-60 [61-62];   7 7/8" x 5 1/4"; printed on wove paper.

Pagination: p. [1] blank, p. [2] blank, p. [3] half-title, p. [4] list of books in series, p. [5] title

page, p. [6] acknowledgments, copyright, p. [7] dedication, p. [8] *"old men carrying their fathers and
philosophers / weeping in the dust, America perhaps,
Don Quixote"* / -- MALCOLM LOWRY, Under the Volcano,
pp. [9-10] introduction by K.S., p. [11] contents, p.
[12] blank, pp. 15-60 text, pp. [61-62] blank.

Binding: Issued in light tan paper over boards. Front
cover: [in red:] INTRODUCTION BY / KARL SHAPIRO [in
script:] Jack Hirschman [publisher's emblem] / [large
drawing of human bodies] / [reading downwards, along
right edge:] a correspondence of Americans. Back
cover: [in red: photograph of Jack Hirschman by Myriam
Champigny] / JACK HIRSCHMAN / [in script:] A Correspondence / of Americans / [twenty-four line note
about the author, including paragraph from introduction by K.S.] / FRONT COVER ILLUSTRATION FROM A DRAW-
ING BY LEON GOLUB / $2.75.

Publication: Published by Indiana University Press,
September 26, 1960, at $2.75.

Contents: 9-10 "Introduction [by K.S.]."

Note: Regarding collation, p. 15 is first numbered
page. Front matter adds up to 12 pp. Thus, pp. 13-
14 were not included.

B9   KARL SHAPIRO A BIBLIOGRAPHY   1960

karl shapiro / *a bibliography* / *by William White* /
[device] / *with a note by* / *Karl Shapiro* / DETROIT
[device] WAYNE STATE UNIVERSITY PRESS [device] 1960

Collation: pp. [i-viii] [1-6] 7-9 [10] 11-69 [70] 71-
105 [106] 107-113 [114-120]; 8 3/4" x 6"; printed
on wove paper.

Pagination: pp. [i-iv] blank, p. [v] THIS COPY OF
KARL SHAPIRO--A BIBLIOGRAPHY / IS PRESENTED TO / [*Mr.
Karl Shapiro*] / WITH THE COMPLIMENTS OF / Mr. Charles

FIVE YOUNG AMERICAN POETS

Second Series 1941

PAUL GOODMAN · JEANNE McGAHEY
CLARK MILLS · DAVID SCHUBERT
KARL SHAPIRO

NEW DIRECTIONS   NORFOLK, CONN.

B1

IN DIFESA DELL'IGNORANZA

CULTURA SOTTO INCHIESTA L'ER
OTICA CONTRO L'ERMENEUTICA
UNA TEORIA DEL PRIMATO DELLA
EMOZIONE NELL'ATTO POETICO
E NELL'ESPERIENZA PERSONALE
DELLA POESIA

KARL
SHAPIRO

LERICI
EDITORE

E24

E. Feinberg / AND / THE MEMBERS OF THE EDITORIAL BOARD
/ OF / THE WAYNE STATE UNIVERSITY PRESS / Benjamin B.
Ashcom / Harold A. Basilius / H. Linn Edsall / Sereck
H. Fox / Sidney Glazer / Robert F. Gleckner / Gabriel
W. Lasker / G. Flint Purdy / David Wineman / DETROIT,
MICHIGAN [device] NOVEMBER 17, 1960, p. [vi] blank, p.
[vii] half-title, pp. [viii-1] blank, p. [2] plate, p.
[3] title page, p. [4] copyright, statement of limitation, p. [5] contents, p. [6] blank, pp. 7-9 text, p.
[10] blank, pp. 11-69 text, p. [70] blank, pp. 71-105
text, p. [106] blank, pp. 107-113 index, p. [114]
blank, p. [115] colophon, pp. [116-120] blank.

Binding: Brown Holliston's Waverly cloth over boards.
Spine stamped in gold, reading downwards: Karl Shapiro
a bibliography [device] *by William White* wayne. Golden
marbled endpapers.

Dust jacket: Issued without dust jacket.

Publication: Published in an edition of one hundred
copies by Wayne State University Press on November 17,
1960. An additional 250 copies bound in Linweave Text
Laid Antique paper covers were issued simultaneously.

Contents: 11-12 "Note by Karl Shapiro."

B10   PROSE KEYS TO MODERN POETRY   1962

[illustration] / Prose Keys to Modern Poetry / *Edited
by* / KARL SHAPIRO / *University of Nebraska* / HARPER &
ROW, PUBLISHERS / New York, Evanston, and London

Collation: pp. [i-iv] v-xii [1-2] 3-160 [161-162] 163-
260; printed on wove paper.

Pagination: p. [i] half-title, p. [ii] blank, p. [iii]
title page, p. [iv] copyright, pp. v-vi acknowledgments, pp. vii-viii foreword, pp. ix-xii contents, p.
[1] half-title, p. [2] blank, pp. 3-160 text, p. [161]
half-title, p. [162] blank, pp. 163-260 text.

Binding: Issued in stiff light green paper covers.
Front: [illustration on left side in green and black]
/ [in green:] Prose / Keys / to / Modern / Poetry /
[in black:] KARL / SHAPIRO. Spine, reading downwards:
[in black:] KARL SHAPIRO [in green: rule] [in white:]
Prose Keys to Modern Poetry / [in green: rule] [in
black:] HARPER / & / ROW. Back cover: ads for other
Harper & Row books.

Publication: Published by Harper & Row, May 14, 1962.

Contents: Edited, with foreword and headnotes, plus a
chronological guide to modern poetry, by K.S.

B11   THE WRITER'S EXPERIENCE   1964

The Writer's / Experience / RALPH ELLISON *and* KARL
SHAPIRO / [Library of Congress emblem] / PUBLISHED
FOR THE / LIBRARY OF CONGRESS / by the Gertrude Clarke
Whittall Poetry and Literature Fund / WASHINGTON: 1964

Collation: pp. [i-ii] iii [iv] v [vi] 1-32 [33-34];
9 1/8" x 5 3/4"; printed on wove paper.

Pagination: p. [i] title page, p. [ii] L.C. card number, publisher's address, price, p. iii statement on
The Gertrude Clarke Whittall Poetry and Literature
Fund, p. [iv] blank, p. v contents, p. [vi] blank, pp.
1-32 text, pp. [33-34] blank.

Binding: Issued in cream and tan paper wrappers,
stapled. Front cover: [in tan:] The Writer's / Experience / RALPH ELLISON *and* KARL SHAPIRO / [decora-
tive rule] / [in cream:] *Lectures Presented Under the
/ Auspices of the Gertrude Clarke Whittall / Poetry
and Literature Fund.* Back cover: decorative rule in
tan. Inside back cover there is a list of other
lectures issued by the Library of Congress in this
series.

Publication: Published by the Gertrude Clarke Whittall

Poetry and Literature Fund for the Library of Congress
in 1964 at 20¢. Printed by the U.S. Government Printing Office, Washington, D.C.

Contents: Contribution by K.S. is 16 "American Poet?"
(Text of a lecture delivered on January 27, 1964, at
the Library of Congress).

B12   A PROSODY HANDBOOK   1965

*A Prosody Handbook / Karl Shapiro / The University of
Nebraska / Robert Beum / The Creighton University /
Harper & Row, Publishers / New York, Evanston, and
London*

Collation: pp. [i-iv] v-x 1-214; 8 1/2" x 5 3/4";
printed on wove paper.

Pagination: p. [i] half-title, p. [ii] blank, p. [iii]
title page, p. [iv] copyright, pp. v-vi acknowledgments, p. vii contents, pp. viii-ix foreword, p. x
note, pp. 1-212 text, pp. 213-214 index.

Binding: Issued in gold cloth over boards. Front
cover: illustration of leaves stamped in gold. Spine,
reading downwards: *A Prosody Handbook Shapiro and Beum
/ Harper & Row.* Golden endpapers.

Dust jacket: Issued in dust jacket. Front cover,
white and gold paper, printing in green: *A Prosody
Handbook / by Karl Shapiro & Robert Beum /* [white
rule] / [illustration of leaves] / *A Manual for the
Poet and the Poetry Lover.* Spine, green paper: [in
white:] *A Prosody Handbook /* [in dark gold:] *by Karl
Shapiro & Robert Beum /* HARPER & ROW. Back cover,
white paper printed in green: *A Prosody Handbook /*
Karl Shapiro & Robert Beum / [from the foreword,
twenty-six lines] / *Harper & Row, Publishers, /* 49
East 33d Street, New York 10016. Flyleaves, white
paper printed in green; contain synopsis of the book
and note on the authors.

Publication: Published by Harper & Row, New York, January 27, 1965, at $4.95.

Contents: viii "Foreword," x "A Note on Terms," 1 "Prosody as a Study," 6 "Poetry and Verse," 8 "Syllables: Color, Stress, Quantity, Pitch," 27 "The Foot," 45 "The Line," 53 "Accentual and Syllabic Verse," 60 "Meter and Rhythm," 66 "The Uses of Meter," 83 "Tempo," 86 "Rhyme," 96 "The Uses of Rhyme," 107 "The Stanza," 111 "Stanza Forms," 135 "The Sonnet," 141 "Blank Verse," 148 "Free Verse," 153 "Classical Prosody," 159 "Prosody and Period," 166 "Scansions and Comments," 181 "Glossary," 203 "A Selected Bibliography," 213 "Index."

B13   HARLEM GALLERY   1965

HARLEM GALLERY / Book I, The Curator / by / M.B. Tolson / *with an introduction by* / KARL SHAPIRO / TWAYNE PUBLISHERS, INC. / NEW YORK

Collation: pp. [1-8] 9-15 [16-18] 19-173 [174-176]; 8 3/8" x 5 3/4"; printed on wove paper.

Pagination: p. [1] half-title, p. [2] other books by Tolson, p. [3] title page, p. [4] copyright, p. [5] dedication, p. [6] blank, p. [7] acknowledgments, p. [8] blank, pp. 9-10 contents, pp. 11-15 introduction, p. [16] blank, p. [17] half-title, p. [18] blank, pp. 19-173 text, pp. [174-76] blank.

Binding: Issued in gray cloth over boards. Front cover: *THE / HARLEM / GALLERY /* Book I: / THE CURATOR / MELVIN B. TOLSON. Spine, reading downwards: Tolson THE HARLEM GALLERY BOOK I: THE CURATOR Twayne. White endpapers.

Dust jacket: Issued in white dust wrapper, with brown and green rectangles on front cover. Front cover: [in black:] M.B. TOLSON / HARLEM / GALLERY / [vertical, in white:] HARLEM GALLERY / [in black:] HARLEM

/ GALLERY / M.B. TOLSON. Spine, printed in green, reading downwards: TOLSON HARLEM GALLERY TWAYNE. Back cover, printed in brown: [photograph of M.B. Tolson] / [note on the author, forty-eight lines] / TWAYNE PUBLISHERS, INC., 31 Union Square West, New York 3, N. Y. Flyleaves printed in brown; contains synopsis of book with selection from "Introduction" by K.S.

Publication: Published by Twayne Publishers, Inc., February 16, 1965, at $4.00. Typesetting by Bardou Linotype Service, Inc.

Contents: 11 "Introduction [by K.S.]."

B14   THE LITTLE MAGAZINE AND CONTEMPORARY LITERATURE
1966

[rule] The Little Magazine / and Contemporary Litera- ture / [rule] A Symposium Held At The / LIBRARY OF CONGRESS / 2 and 3 April 1965 / [rule] / Published for the / Reference Department / Library of Congress / by the / Modern Language Association of America / 1966

Collation: pp. [i-iv] v-vi [vii-viii] [1-2] 3-38 [39-40] 41-73 [74-76] 77-117 [118] 119 [120]; 9" x 6"; printed on wove paper.

Pagination: p. [i] half-title, p. [ii] blank, p. [iii] title page, p. [iv] copyright, pp. v-vi foreword, p. [vii] contents, p. [viii] blank, p. [1] half-title, p. [2] blank, pp. 3-38 text, p. [39] half-title, p. [40] blank, pp. 41-73 text, p. [74] blank, p. [75] half-title, p. [76] blank, pp. 77-117 text, p. [118] blank, p. 119 index, p. [120] blank.

Binding: Issued in white paper covers. Front cover: white letters on green background: *The / Little / Magazine / and / Contemporary / Literature* / [in black:] Modern Language Association of America. Spine: [in black:] The Little Magazine and Contempor- ary Literature [in green:] MLA.

Publication: Published for the Reference Department,
Library of Congress, by the Modern Language Association of America at $1.25.

Contents: 15-20 "The Campus Literary Organ," 21-38
"Discussion" [with Reed Whittemore, Jules Chametzky,
William Phillips, Karl Shapiro, Henry Rago, Theodore
Weiss, and members of the audience].

B15   A LOCAL HABITATION & A NAME   1974

A local / habitation [decorative:] & a name / poems
by / Ted / Kooser

Collation: pp. [i-xiv] 1-57 [58] 59-79 [80-82]; 8 3/8"
x 5 3/8"; printed on wove paper.

Pagination: pp. [i-ii] blank, brown paper, p. [iii]
title page, p. [iv] copyright, acknowledgments, publisher's address, p. [v] dedication, p. [vi] blank,
pp. [vii-viii] contents, p. [ix] introduction by K.S.,
p. [x] blank, pp. [xi-xii] blank, brown paper, p.
[xiii] half-title, p. [xiv] blank, pp. 1-56 text, p.
57 half-title, p. [58] blank, pp. 59-79 text, pp.
[80-81] blank, p. [82] note on the author.

Binding: Issued in cream-colored paper wrappers.
Front: [in brown:] / A local / habitation [decorative,
brown & gold:] & [in brown:] a name / [in gold:] poems
by / [in brown:] Ted / Kooser / [in gold: illustra-
tion]. Spine, reading downwards on brown paper: [in
cream:] A local habitation & a name [in gold:] Ted
Kooser [cream squares, in gold:] SOLO PRESS. Back
cover: photograph of the author by John Spence. Designed by Peter Langmack.

Publication: Published by Solo Press, San Luis Obispo,
California, September 12, 1974.

Contents: [ix] " Introduction [by K.S.]."

B16 TRYNE   1976

TRYNE / by / Cynthia Bates / Steve Ellzey / Bill Lynch
/ Copyright 1976

Collation: pp. [1-48].

Pagination: pp. [1-2] blank, p. [3] title page, p. [4]
acknowledgments, p. [5] dedication, pp. [6-7] contents,
p. [8] blank, p. [9] illustration, p. [10] blank, pp.
[11-19] text, p. [20] blank, p. [21] illustration, p.
[22] blank, pp. [23-32] text, p. [33] illustration,
p. [34] blank, pp. [35-44] text, pp. [45-48] blank.

Binding: Issued in olive paper wrappers, stapled.
Front cover: illustration by Michael Houston; in
rectangle, center of illustration: TRYNE / [rule] /
Karl / Shapiro, editor.

Publication: Published in 1976 by the authors. Title
page signed by K.S. below copyright.

Contents: Student work, edited by K.S.

C. CONTRIBUTIONS TO PERIODICALS

1933

C1   *Article:* "From the Catechuman: A First Year Man's Philosophy," *University of Virginia Magazine* (1932-33), 34.

1939

C2   *Poem:* "Property," *The New Anvil*, I (December, 1939), 22.

C3   *Poems:* "To a Guineapig," "Self-History," *Poetry World* (December, 1939), 15-16.

1940

C4   *Poem:* "Self-History," *Herald* [Sanford, Florida] (January 31, 1940). According to William White, reprinted in *Knickerbocker News* [Albany, New York] (February 2, 1940), *Mail* [Charleston, West Virginia] (February, 1940), *News* [Lynchburg, Virginia] (February, 1940), and *News* [Newport, Rhode Island] (February, 1940).

C5   *Poem:* "Death of Emma Goldman," *Partisan Review*, VII (July-August, 1940), 267.

C6   *Poems:* "University," "Midnight Show," "Love Poem," "Necropolis," *Poetry*, LVII (October, 1940), 24-29.

1941

C7   *Poem:* "How Long Ago the Home," *The Nation*, CLII (January, 1941), 48.

C8   *Poem:* "Washington Cathedral," *Partisan Review*, VIII (March-April, 1941), 94-95.

C9   *Review:* "Two Veterans," *Poetry*, LVIII (May, 1941), 100-102.

A review of *Poems 1930-40* by Edmund Blunden, and *Rhymed Ruminations* by Siegfried Sassoon. "From the standpoint of most young writers of this decade, two things are immediately apparent about these works: (1) they have a currency they do not deserve; (2) they continue to defy the 'progress' of modern poetry.... To the present generation of war writers this is a very tame promise indeed."

C10   *Poems:* "Hospital," "Pharmacy," "The Snob," "Mongolian Idiot," "Scyros," "The Contraband," "My Grandmother," *Poetry*, LVIII (July, 1941), 175-182.

C11   *Review:* "Symbol of Our Search," *Poetry*, LVIII (August, 1941), 264-266.

A review of *The Airmen* by Selden Rodman. "That the poet must be the scholar of his own work is one of the characteristic vices of modern writing and accounts in part for the elephantiasis of many of our poems. Of this disorder, photography, source-notes, marginalia, and diagrams, on the one hand, and multiple metrical forms and a variety of styles on the other, are typical symptoms.... Mr. Rodman's long poem, *The Airmen*, is relatively free of the imperfections of its form.... *The Airmen*, at any rate, is a political poem and as such is open to political examination. There is little question that Mr. Rodman's moral efforts confuse the great issue of his poem."

C12   *Review:* "De Imitatione," *Poetry*, LVIII (September, 1941), 340-343.

A review of *The End of the Decade* by Harry Brown, *Shadow on the Sun* by Robert Friend, and *The Metaphor in the Jungle* by Parker Tyler. Explores the question of poetic influence, concluding "they approve the idea that something can be

assimilated from somebody and reproduced without
counterfeiting."

C13   *Letter:* "Letters from the Army," *Partisan Review*,
        VIII (September-October, 1941), 439.

        A letter to Dwight Macdonald. "I've changed my
        mind about the Army letter I agreed to write for
        P.R.... Maybe I've been eating lotus--I don't
        know, but very likely my imagination has been
        corrected by a dish of cabbage.... The claims
        of the Government about good treatment are sub-
        stantially true."

C14   *Poems:* "Conscription Camp," "A Robbery," "October
        1," *Poetry*, LIX (November, 1941), 66-71.

C15   *Poem:* "The Contraband," *Niagara Falls Gazette*
        (December 6, 1941).

                            1942

C16   *Poems:* "Terminal," "Newsboy," "Waitress," "Trav-
        elogue for Exiles," "Going to the War," *Poetry*,
        LX (May, 1942), 57-62.

C17   *Letter:* "Dear Miss Crozier," *A Comment*, No. 12
        (July, 1942), 2.

        A letter to Cecily Crozier, editor of the Aus-
        tralian *A Comment* and publisher in 1942 of A2.
        "In the land of Bing and Garbo, Einstein, Mann,
        Popeye, and Eleanor, A COMMENT would be first
        class. Except for VIEW and PARTISAN REVIEW of
        Greenwich Village, nothing can touch it.... The
        official literati such as the Librarian MacLeish
        and the professor Van Wych [sic] Brooks have
        launched a savage assault against 'the coterie'
        of Rimbaud, Valery, Joyce, Proust, Eliot, Heming-
        way, etc. etc., striking at the very roots of
        last generation Modernism.... The better Uni-

versity Quarterlies, KENYON REVIEW and SOUTHERN
REVIEW, have developed a warped metaphysical jar-
gon and a corrupt prose that threaten to scare
poetry and criticism alike off the map.... The
Neo-Classic malaise has broken out. Auden, back
in England, seems a likely candidate for the
Laureateship—almost anything he has written
since 1939 would fit into Quiller-Couch.... All
of the stale battles of the '20's and '30's have
to be fought over again."

C18   *Poems:* "The Mother," "War Poem," *A Comment*, No.
       12 (July, 1942), 4, 17.

C19   *Poem:* "Haircut," *Partisan Review*, IX (July-Au-
       gust, 1942), 393.

C20   *Poems:* "Paradox: The Birds," "Epitaph for John
       and Richard," *Common Sense*, XI (September, 1942),
       302-303.

C21   *Poems:* "Giantess," "Les Aveugles," "The Vigil,"
       A Comment, No. 13 (October, 1942), 4, 5, 20.

C22   *Poems:* "Ballade of the Second-Best Bed," "The
       Twins," "A Cut Flower," "Nostalgia," *Poetry*, LXI
       (November, 1942), 411-416.

C23   *Poems:* "Five Lyrics" ["I Sing the Simplest Flow-
       er," "Dark Words, Birds of the Race," "The
       Soldier's Death Occasions," "Treasure Your
       Anonymity," "Witty of Heart and Pure of Heart"],
       Harper's, CLXXXVI (December, 1942), 28-29.

                          1943

C24   *Poems:* "The Voyage," "Mutability," "Hill at Par-
       ramatta," *A Comment*, No. 14 (January, 1943), 9,
       10, 18.

C25   *Poem:* "Satire: Anxiety," *Chimera*, I (Winter,
       1943), 3-4.

C26   *Poem:* "Hill at Parramatta," *Contemporary Poetry*, II (Winter, 1943), 5.

C27   *Poems:* "The New Ring," "The Immaterial Joy," *A Comment*, No. 15 (March, 1943), 11, 18, 19.

C28   *Poem:* "The Bridge," *Harper's*, CLXXXVI (April, 1943), 463.

C29   *Poem:* "The Gun," *Common Sense*, XII (May, 1943), 173.

C30   *Poem:* "New Guinea," *The Nation*, CLVI (May 8, 1943), 671.

C31   omitted

C32   *Poem:* "D.H.L.," *Harper's*, CLXXXVII (June, 1943), 43.

C33   *Poem:* "Love Letter (by V-Mail from Australia)," *The New Yorker*, XIX (June 12, 1943), 24.

C34   *Poem:* "Magician," *Meanjin Papers*, II (Summer, 1943), 18.

C35   *Article:* "Soldiers Speak," *Common Sense*, XII (July, 1943), 257.

C36   *Poems:* "A Cut Flower," "Portrait of My Head," "Comedian," *A Comment*, No. 16 (July, 1943), 16, 17, 19, 20.

C37   *Poem:* "Full Moon: New Guinea," *Common Sense*, XII (July, 1943), 46.

C38   *Poem:* "New Guinea Letter," *The New Republic*, CIX (July 12, 1943), 46.

C39   *Poem:* "The Synagogue," *Partisan Review*, X (July-August, 1943), 317-319.

C40   *Poem:* "Fireworks," *Contemporary Poetry*, III (Autumn, 1943), 9.

C41   *Poems:* "Paris," "Nigger," "Lord, I Have Seen Too
      Much," "Movie Actress," "Jew," "Red Indian,"
      "Jefferson," *Poetry*, LXII (August, 1943), 237-
      246.

C42   *Poem:* "Troop Train," *The New Republic*, CIX
      (August 23, 1943), 252.

C43   *Poem:* "Troop Train," *Meanjin Papers*, II (Autumn,
      1943), 8.

C44   *Poem:* "Public Library," *Baltimore Evening Sun*
      (August 30, 1943), 17.

C45   *Poem:* "The Natives," *A Comment*, No. 17 (October,
      1943), 13, 14.

C46   *Poem:* "Sunday: New Guinea," *Good Housekeeping*,
      117 (November, 1943), 48.

C47   *Poems:* "The Play," "Babel," *Southerly*, IV (December, 1943), 11-13.

C48   *Poem:* "Christmas Tree," *Poetry*, LXIII (December,
      1943), 148-149.

C49   *Poem:* "Christmas Eve (Australia, 1943)," *The New
      Yorker*, XIX (December 25, 1943), 26.

1944

C50   *Poem:* "Elegy for a Dead Soldier," *The New Republic*, CX (January 10, 1944), 50-51.

C51   *Poem:* "The Intellectual," *Partisan Review*, XI
      (Winter, 1944), 43-44.

C52   *Poems:* " The Natives," "Comedian," *Maryland
      Quarterly*, No. 2 (1944), 40-42.

C53   *Poem:* "Aside," *Mademoiselle*, XVIII (March, 1944),
      139.

C54   *Poems:* "Five Poems" ["The Puritan," "The Inter-
      lude," "Ballet Mecanique," "Shylock," "The Leg"],
      Poetry, LXIII (March, 1944), 299-305.

C55   *Poem:* "The Bed," *The New Yorker*, XX (April 22,
      1944), 26.

C56   *Poem:* "The Puritan," *Meanjin Papers*, III (Autumn,
      1944), 28.

C57   *Poem:* "Public Library," *New York Public Library,
      Branch Library Book News*, XXI (October, 1944),
      117.

C58   *Poems:* "Public Library," "Crusoe," *Southerly*,
      V, 1 (1944), 4, 25.

                          1945

C59   *Poem:* "On Reading Keats in Wartime," *The New York
      Times Book Review*, L (February 11, 1945), 2.

C60   *Poem:* "Crusoe," *The New York Times Book Review*,
      L (April 29, 1945), 2.

C61   *Poem:* "Honeymoon," *The New Yorker*, XXI (June 23,
      1945), 28.

C62   *Poem:* from "Essay on Rime," *Kenyon Review*, VII
      (Summer, 1945), 378-381.

C63   *Poem:* "Essay on Rime," ["Dialectic and Criticism,"
      "Dead Hand and Exhaustion of Our Rime"], *Poetry*,
      LXVI (July, 1945), 197-203.

C64   *Poem:* "Homecoming," *The New Yorker*, XXI (August
      18, 1945), 28.

C65   *Article:* "A Poet Dissects the Modern Poets,"
      New York Times Magazine (September 23, 1945),
      45-46.

"If one could write the typical composite poem
of the present day, the finished product would
appear to be a work of great intricacy of device
from thirty to fifty lines in length, easy to
read, but difficult to comprehend.... Our poem
would be anti-lyrical in tone, anti-romantic in
spirit, and in point of view probably anti-
middle class.... The poem would appear in a
liberal magazine, a literary journal or quarterly review and would eventually finds [sic] its
way to three or four American and one English
anthology. About 5,000 people, mostly poets
and college students, would read it. Its life
expectancy would be about five or ten years....
The landscape of modern poetry shows a highly
urbanized, quiescent and intent company, at odds
with man's condition and the state--a company
whose single great reverence is for the poet's
art. From this scene our composite poet looks
out upon a new post-war world and probably tries
to judge his potential relationship with his
civilization which has so narrowly escaped with
its life. And very probably, although he is at
bottom as thankful as the next man, he is not
yet ready to turn his thanks into praise."

C66   *Poem:* "Troop Train," *Scholastic*, XLVII (October
      1, 1945), 19.

C67   *Poem:* "The Confusion in Language: General and
      Personal Idiom," *Sewanee Review*, LIII (October,
      1945), 580-585.

C68   *Poem:* "Connecticut Valley," *The New Yorker*, XXI
      (November 3, 1945), 34.

C69   *Article:* "The Jewish Writer," *New Masses*, LVII
      (November 6, 1945), 23-24.

      Response to Nathan Ausbel's article "The Jewish
      Writer's Dilemma." "I am Jewish and I am a
      writer but I do not consider myself, and am not
      considered, a 'Jewish writer.'... I don't think

the writer who happens to be a Jew has any more
obligation to his Jewishness than a Christian
writer has to his Christianness.... It would be
well to remember that the Jews who perished in
Germany were victims and not slaughtered saints.
I do not think it is fitting for a Jewish writer
to isolate the Jews from the other, more numerous,
victims of Hitlerism."

C70   *Poem:* "He-Man," *The New Yorker*, XXI (December 1,
1945), 42.

C71   *Letter:* "Arguments on Rime: Karl Shapiro Objects,"
The Nation, CLX (December 22, 1945), 690-692.

A response to Delmore Schwartz's review of "Essay
on Rime" in *The Nation* of November 10, 1945. K.S.
responds to seven points made by Schwartz and
concludes, "I would like to register a protest
with *The Nation*'s literary editor for printing
a piece of criticism as invidious and deliberately falsified as Delmore Schwartz's review....
There seems to be a slump in the art of book reviewing when the personal rancor of an embittered
young man passes for literary judgement in the
pages of *The Nation*." Delmore Schwartz's response follows this letter.

1946

C72   *Poem:* "Demobilization," *The New Yorker*, XXII
(February 16, 1946), 32.

C73   *Poem:* "News to Australia," *Meanjin Papers*, V
(Spring, 1946), 215-218.

C74   *Poem:* "The Travelers," *Chicago Review*, I (Spring,
1946), 69.

C75   *Article:* "The Bohemian," *Wake*, I (Spring, 1946),
45.

C76   *Poem:* "The Convert," *The New Yorker*, XXII (April 13, 1946), 38.

C77   *Poem:* "The Progress of Faust," *The New Yorker*, XXII (May 11, 1946), 28.

C78   *Poem:* "News to Australia," *The New Republic*, CXIV (June 3, 1946), 808.

C79   *Poem:* "In the Waxworks," *The Nation*, CLXIII (July 20, 1946), 74.

C80   *Poem:* "Poets of Hell," *The New Yorker*, XXII (November 23, 1946), 38.

C81   *Poem:* "Recapitulations," *Poetry*, LXIX (December, 1946), 121-133.

1947

C82   *Poem:* "Boy-Man," *The New Yorker*, XXII (January 11, 1947), 26.

C83   *Article:* "A Note on American Poetry," *Poetry*, LXIX (February, 1947), 273-275.

In January, 1947, the French National Radio initiated a series of programs on "Les rapports existant entre les litteratures contemporaines et francaise." This "Note" by K.S. was written for that broadcast. "It seems to me that the central argument of American poetry is, and to a certain extent always has been, whether to accept or to reject America.... For my own part, although I cannot see how America will ever create a great poetry unless it can stop the flow of American talent toward Europe. And I cannot see how we can arrest this flow until our poets establish some equilibrium between themselves and the nation.... I cannot say whether we shall ever have another Poe, but this is what we need,

--a spirit to lead us not to and fro in the land but into our own special genius."

C84 *Poem:* "Air-Liner," *The New Yorker*, XXIII (May 10, 1947), 36.

C85 *Poem:* "D.C.," *The New Yorker*, XXIII (May 24, 1947), 38.

C86 *Article:* "English Prosody and Modern Poetry," *ELH*, XIV (June, 1947), 77-92.

   First publication of A6. Given as the annual Tudor and Stuart Club Lecture, April 18, 1947.

C87 *Poem:* "Words for a Child's Birthday," *The New Yorker*, XXIII (June 28, 1947), 32.

C88 *Poem:* "A Song of Conscience," *The New Yorker*, XXIII (July 26, 1947), 26.

C89 *Poems:* "Attentions of Hymen," "The Dirty Word," "The Cross-Tree," *Poetry*, LXX (August, 1947), 233-237.

C90 *Poem:* "The Southerner," *The New Yorker*, XXIII (September 27, 1947), 38.

C91 *Poem:* "An Urn of Ashes," *Poetry Quarterly*, IX (Autumn, 1947), 162.

1948

C92 *Article:* "A Farewell to Criticism," *Poetry*, LXXI (January, 1948), 196-217.

   Text of the William Vaughn Moody Lecture given by K.S. at the University of Chicago, November 13, 1947. "How criticism has undertaken to be the strongest authority for the reading and writing of a poem is not my question; my question is

merely the contention that it has.... A poem is
not really assisted by criticism, either before
or after its completion.... There is only one
species of critic who can infiltrate my confidence sufficiently to make me lose myself in
what he has to say: he is the humanist critic,
a name I would broaden to include such writers
as Sainte-Beuve, Saintsbury, and Longinus. I
mean the critic whose love of poetry exceeds any
infatuation with a theory of poetry or any con-
cern with a purely scientific motive.... Poetry
cannot be understood; it can only be reacted to."

C93   *Poem:* "The Minute," *The Nation*, CLXVI (January
      17, 1948), 76.

C94   *Poem:* "Ballade of the Critic," *The New Yorker*,
      XXIV (June 5, 1948), 39.

C95   *Poem:* "Israfel," *The New Yorker*, XXIV (June 12,
      1948), 28. Reprinted in *Congress Bulletin* [Amer-
      ican Jewish Congress] (October 7, 1948).

C96   *Poem:* "The Tingling Back," *Botteghe Oscure*, II
      (1948), 292-293.

                          1949

C97   *Article:* "Prosody as the Meaning," *Poetry*, LXXIII,
      (March, 1949), 336-351.

      "My chief motive behind this paper is to convince
      the reader of poetry and the poet himself that
      criticism is not essential to the artistic geni-
      us of the poet or to the artistic genius of the
      audience.... It seems to me that criticism,
      however scientific or intuitive it may be, can
      discover only secondary data about art, whereas
      the primary data are wholly contained in the
      work of art and proceed in a straight line from
      the object to the subject.... There are three

statements I wish to make about the scope of
prosody: (1) that every poem has a discoverable
organization; (2) that the poet is only slightly
more aware of this organization than the reader;
(3) that the intimate knowledge of this total
structure does not necessarily contribute to
what we call our appreciation of the poem....
Criticism, however richly it may inform the
judgement, must always defer to a more instinc-
tive source in the mind; and the fact of liking
must remain the supreme touchstone of the work
of art."

C98   *Poem:* "The Doorman," *The New Yorker*, XXV (March
       19, 1949), 32.

C99   *Article:* "The Question of the Pound Award," *Par-
       tisan Review*, XVI (May, 1949), 512-522.

       "I voted against Pound in the balloting for the
       Bollingen Prize. My first and more crucial rea-
       son was that I am a Jew and cannot honor anti-
       semites. My second reason I stated in a report
       which was circulated among the Fellows: 'I voted
       against Pound in the belief that the poet's
       political and moral philosophy ultimately viti-
       ates his poetry and lowers its standard as liter-
       ary work....' Through his experience with vi-
       cious and ugly ideas, what poetic insights into
       our world has this poet given us? Pound's work
       as a poet rests upon some answer to such a ques-
       tion.... The technical charge of treason against
       Pound is not our concern, but all artists should
       stand against this poet for his greater crime
       against civilization."

C100   *Article:* "Case History of 'The Minute,'" *Hopkins
       Review*, II (Summer, 1949), 3-9.

C101   *Poem:* "Going to School," *Partisan Review*, XVI
       (September, 1949), 921-923.

C102   *Article:* "The Jewish Writer and the English Literary Tradition," *Commentary*, VII (October, 1949), 369-370.

Part of a symposium on "the sinister Jew in English Literature." "I am foreign matter to the European tradition of life and letters, and if I do not believe in a new and separate American civilization, I shall have no other cultural identity.... I have always been able to 'understand' Chaucerian even Shakespearean anti-Semitism as lingering concepts of the medieval mind. Naturally, I make no such concessions to the modern literary anti-Semite, however great an artist he happens to be.... When Eliot perpetuates the myth of the bestial Jew, without taking the pains elsewhere to mollify this image, he commits an outrage against his Jewish contemporaries."

C103   *Poem:* "The Tooth and the Trout," *Hopkins Review*, II (Winter, 1949), 48.

1950

C104   *Article:* "What Is Anti-Criticism?" *Poetry*, LXXXV, (March, 1950), 339-351.

Text of a lecture delivered by K.S. at C.C.N.Y. (October, 1949), Brandeis University (November, 1949), St. John's College (November, 1949), American University (December, 1949). "This lecture is intended as a general defense of criticism and a specific defense of contemporary poetics. I shall defend, lawyer style, interpretive criticism, literary coteries, the select audience, estheticism so called, and obscurity so called. I shall deprecate the idea of a great audience, mass culture, and the esthetic of the American middle class. My object is to show that the argument against criticism, a small and special hypothesis at most, is related to a

wider and more dangerous anti-intellectualism
that in poetics leads to the primacy of the
second-rate, and that in literary politics may
lead to official and controlled art."

C105 *Poem:* "The Figurehead," *Botteghe Oscure*, VI
(1950), 450-451.

1951

C106 *Poem:* "Carte Postale," *Western Review*, XVI
(Autumn, 1951), 32.

C107 *Poems:* "Eden Retold": "The Sickness of Adam,"
"The Recognition of Eve," "The Kiss," "The Tree
of Guilt," "The Confession," "Shame," "Exile,"
Poetry, LXXVIII (July, 1951), 187-196.

1952

C108 *Poem:* "Homage to Calder," *The New Yorker*, XXVIII
(March 29, 1952), 34.

C109 *Article:* "Poets and Psychologists," *Poetry*, LXXX
(June, 1952), 166-184.

"About a year ago I received an invitation from
a psychologist to be examined on my imaginative
powers.... The psychologist was bound to enter
the field of poetry (everything being a field).
He has more tests up his sleeve than you can
count; his statistics are probably foolproof,
and his objectivity is perfect. But he won't
find a thing." Pages 169-183 contain the psychologist's questions and K.S.'s responses, ending with a discussion of Pound and the Bollingen
Award. "My position was that this poet's political and moral views seemed to me to vitiate his
poetry and ultimately lower its esthetic value.

Otherwise I can only say that the book the *Pisan Cantos was* the best book of verse of that year, and of many years, and that I have always been an admirer of Pound's poetry.... It seems to me that psychology is one of those sciences that was born out of the ruins of literature, and it is necessary to our world *because* literature is no longer central to our spiritual life."

C110 *Poem:* "Anniversary for F.O. Matthiessen," *Poetry*, LXXXI (October, 1952), 69-70.

C111 *Poem:* "Love for a Hand," *The New Yorker*, XXVIII (October 4, 1952), 38.

1953

C112 *Poem:* "The Phenomenon," *The New Yorker*, XXVIII (February 7, 1953), 34.

C113 *Articles:* "Library Notes," *Newberry Library Bulletin*, III (April, 1953), 61-72.

This and the following nine items are ephemeral pieces written by K.S. while editor of the *Newberry Library Bulletin*: "The Third Newberry Library Conference on American Studies," III (June, 1953), 73-87; "William Brooks Greenlee (1872-1953)," III (June, 1953), 93; "Library Notes," III (June, 1953), 101-108; "Little Magazines in the Newberry," III (October, 1953), 122-126; "The Fourth Newberry Library Conference on American Studies," III (October, 1953), 127-135; "Library Notes," III (October, 1953), 136; "The Arbatsky Collection," III (July, 1954), 170-176; "The Second Newberry Conference on English Historical Studies," III (July, 1954), 189-197; "Library Notes," III (July, 1954), 198-200.

C114 *Article:* "Does *Poetry* Have a 'Policy'?" *Poetry*, LXXXII (June, 1953), 178-180.

1954

C115   *Poem:* "The Alphabet," *Poetry*, LXXXIII (March, 1954), 315.

C116   *Poem:* "Bathers," *The New Yorker*, XXX (August 14, 1954), 22.

C117   *Poem:* "New Museum," *The New Yorker*, XXX (October 9, 1954), 34.

C118   *Poem:* "Poetry Reading," *The New Yorker*, XXX (December 11, 1954), 42.

C119   *Story:* "An Incident in a Castle," *Botteghe Oscure*, XIV (1954), 227-235.

1955

C120   *Article:* "Brassai: Poetic Focus on France," *Art News*, LIII (February, 1955), 46-47, 69-70.

"Photography, which progressed largely through amateur experimentation, suffers from the success of amateurs. And it suffers from the camera it- self.... The camera has an enormous literary appetite; it takes a strong hand to keep it from dawdling or browsing or chattering about trivia. One sometimes can see the struggle between the photographer of genius and his gossiping machine. The wittiness of the finest photography is one of the results of this tussle. The Brassai exhibition (which opened at the Chicago Art Institute, and is now at the Walker Art Center, Minneapolis) proves the point admirably. Nothing is humorous, obvious or cute: everything criti- cizes itself.... The best Brassais, there are enough of them to fix this artist in one's mind permanently, are what appear to be chance, still shots."

C121   *Review:* "W. H. Auden Versus ...," *The New York Times Book Review* (February 20, 1955), 6.

Review of *The Shield of Achilles* by W. H. Auden. "Auden is the Great Ruminator of modern poetry. In many ways he is also the typical poet of our age. In him are the rare words no one really wants to look up. In him are the negative convictions which are the trade-mark of modernism. Over most of the land of modern poetry he maintains his grumpy proprietorship. His whole work is a schoolroom, his universe filled in with phyla, genera and species--all human types.... His main theme is the quest for the Authentic City, a city neither in heaven nor earth, not the Unreal City and not the Accursed City of the self-damned poets, but the city in which human excellence is possible."

C122   *Review:* "In the Forests of the Little People," *The New York Times Book Review* (March 13, 1955), 4.

Review of *Selected Poems* by Randall Jarrell. "In some of Jarrell's writing, criticism and fiction as well as poetry, there is a tendency toward sentimentality and cruelty, but in the major part--and the major part is certainly the poetry--there is a breadth of spirit which is wholly admirable and exemplary. This is a book which should certainly influence our poetry for the better. It should become a point of reference, not only for younger poets, but for all readers of twentieth-century poetry."

C123   *Review:* "The Truth Outside the Rules," *Encounter*, IV (May, 1955), 87-88.

"In these days of collected editions of the most famous English and American poets, one feels a sense of culmination and finality.... As each poet displays his book we are reminded of the incredible riches and the incredible wreckage of

our age. Modern literature is a kind of Last
Judgement in which our acts are sorted out and
pondered. The prescience of ruin, the crackpot
theories, the prayers, the records of our personal grief--these have been the subjects of our
poems.... Spender, MacNeice, Day Lewis, and
Dylan Thomas--who belongs with this group--repre-
sent the best of what we have of the human poets
of our century." Piece continues with a review
of *Autumn Sequel* by Louis MacNeice, *Collected
Poems 1954* by C. Day Lewis, and *Collected Poems
1928-1953* by Stephen Spender.

C124   *Article:* "Dylan Thomas," *Poetry*, LXXXVII (Novem-
       ber, 1955), 100-110.

"The death of Dylan Thomas a year and a half ago
was the cause of the most singular demonstration
of suffering in recent literary history.... When
he died, it was as if there would never be any
more youth in the world. Or so it seemed in the
frenzy of his year-long funeral, a funeral which,
like one of Thomas' own poems, turned slowly into
a satanic celebration and a literary institution.
... Thomas was the first modern romantic you
could put your finger on, the first whose jour-
neys and itineraries became part of his own myth-
ology, the first who offered himself up as a public sacrifice.... Thomas is in somewhat the relation to modern poetry that Hopkins was to
Tennyson and the Victorians; this is a relation
of anti-magnetism. Thomas resisted the literary
traditionalism of the Eliot school; he wanted no
part of it. Poetry to him was not a civilizing
maneuver, a replanting of the gardens; it was a
holocaust, a sowing of the wind.... I went
through the *Collected Poems* recently to decide
which poems I would keep if I were editing the
best poems of Dylan Thomas. Out of about ninety
poems I chose more than thirty which I think
stand with the best poems of our time."

1956

C125 *Letter:* "Karl Shapiro Challenges Graves," *The New Republic*, CXXXIV (April 2, 1956), 3, 23.

A response to Robert Graves' "These Be Thy Gods, O Israel," (*NR*, CXXXIV, February 27, March 5, 1956). "In the interests of literary decency I would like to add one more objection to Graves: his little asides about the drinking and sexual habits of the five idols. The five idols he would like to topple (Thomas, Yeats, Auden, Pound, Eliot) he succeeds only in obscuring temporarily with cigar smoke.... One reason why modern poetry has succeeded as well as it has is that modern prose has so often been thoughtful enough and well-written enough to convince reluctant readers of the merits of its gods.... It is up to Graves and anyone else who assails the altars to provide either better poetry or better criticism than the idols he attacks."

C126 *Poem:* "Photographs of the Poets," *The New Yorker*, XXXII (June 2, 1956), 36.

C127 *Poem:* "In India," *The New Yorker*, XXXII (September 22, 1956), 42.

C128 *Poem:* "Messias," *Poetry London-New York*, I (Winter, 1956), 32-33.

C129 *Article:* "Editorial," *Prairie Schooner*, XXX (Winter, 1956), 309-311.

Written on becoming editor of *PS*. "In the true literary magazine it is the successes and not the failures that count, and questions of consistency of tone and a median style do not prevail. Many an editor of a little magazine has blushed for his contributors—and printed them. For he is on the lookout for a breakthrough, the next turn of the wheel, the door that will open on a different vista.... He does not, of course, turn his back on the famous; he cannot do without them any more than the *New Yorker* can do without advertisers. But it is the new writer he dreams of." Note: as editor, K.S. wrote many of the "Notes on Contributors" for *Prairie Schooner*.

1957

C130 *Poem:* "California Winter," *The New Yorker*, XXXII (January 26, 1957), 33.

C131 *Review:* "Poetry in 1956," *Prairie Schooner*, XXXI (Spring, 1957), 11-16.

Review of *In Defense of the Earth* by Kenneth Rexroth ("He is a warm-blooded, hot-headed poet, and we can forgive him much"); *New and Selected Poems* by Kenneth Fearing ("Fearing is a good poet and in some unexpected way, a direct descendent from Whitman.... But he argues and argues and argues and tires himself out and leaves us wanting to write him a note of congratulation and condolence"); *Collected Poems* by Edna St. Vincent Millay ("I look in vain for the time when men will be so civilized as to appreciate this poet who wrote so voluminously and so passionately and so expertly, almost to no avail"); *Poems of Catullus* by Horace Gregory ("His Catullus is one of the very few examples of a full translation from an ancient poet in which that poet is brought back from the grave and from the classroom"); *Poems from the Greek Anthology* by Dudley Fitts ("His trouble ... is that he is too pious about his originals to allow himself to write a poem"); *Stanzas in Meditation* by Gertrude Stein ("Gertrude Stein was nothing if not proper and correct--she was a great pedant, in fact--and she was on bad terms with the Imagination. She wrote as a poet would if a poet never had a dream or a sleepless night. Somebody (Yale) is trying to make Gertrude out as a poet; and the poets will be getting out their rubber hoses"); and *The Cultivation of Christmas Trees* by T.S. Eliot ("The scholars can leave their picks and shovels in the shed for this one.... Nowadays Eliot has the rectitude and the half-shut eyes of Buddha, and he is purring like a Bunsen burner. And who can say that he has not earned this bliss?").

C132 *Article:* "The Careful Young Men: Tomorrow's Leaders Analyzed by Today's Teachers," *Nation*, CLXXXIV (March 9, 1957), 208.

"When I read your question, a phrase popped into my mind: the Brain-Washed Generation.... As a teacher, I worry about the condition of youth, and I think of the causes. There are three at least: loss of political idealism, the contemporaneity of cultural values, and prosperity.... I wish I could find a student who yells that he hates T.S. Eliot.... May I permit myself one dogmatic remark about books of this generation? It is that one of the most important works of the twentieth century is the textbook called *Understanding Poetry*. It is the book that took poetry off the street and put it in the laboratory. It has not only revolutionized the teaching of literature; it has practically put a stop to genius."

C133 *Poem:* "The House," *Poems in Folio*, I (June, 1957).

C134 *Poems:* "Poems of a Jew" ("Teasing the Nuns," "The First Time," "The Crucifix in the Filing Cabinet," "The Olive Tree," "151st Psalm"), *Poetry*, XC (August, 1957), 265-269.

C135 *Review:* "W. H. Auden: A Leave-Taking," *Prairie Schooner*, XXXI (Summer, 1957), 164-167.

Review of *The Faber Book of Modern American Verse*, edited by W.H. Auden. "The book itself,

without its introduction, is less useful than
most 'treasuries' of verse.... Auden is one of
the long line of the intellectually self-betrayed
of our century, and he has suffered what to him
must be the supreme penalty, the loss of his
audience.... The tremendous stylistic achievement of Auden, comparable to the 'modernizing'
influence of Chaucer or Wordsworth, gives him
his niche in the Abbey. But almost from the
outset of his career, the sensitive poets and
the keenest critics have played the game of taking another 'slap at Auden.' It is the kind of
treatment Eliot, Pound, Stevens, and many others
of lesser gifts have not had to sustain.... Like
his favorite image of the voyager, Auden is once
again on the high seas with his mal de mer."

C136   *Article:* "Romanticism Comes Home," *Prairie Schooner*, XXXI (Fall, 1957), 182-183.

"The San Francisco School of writers ... is the
first symptom of widespread literary revolt to
appear before the walls of modern literary con-
servatism and the Tradition. Hart Crane and
Dylan Thomas belong to their number; the Eliot
citadel and the literature of the academy are
their special targets. But the group has an in-
trinsic significance: it has drawn talent to its
side. The poet Allen Ginsberg and the novelist
Jack Kerouac are the most exciting new names.
Brother Antoninus (William Everson) and Jack
Spicer are just as impressive.... Each age takes
down the masterpieces of its fathers and stores
them in the cellar where someday they will be
exhumed by other judges. In San Francisco they
are building the crates."

C137   *Poem:* "Cadillac," *Hudson Review*, X (Winter, 1957),
541-542.

C138   *Review:* "Poets of the Silent Generation," *Prairie
Schooner*, XXXI (Winter, 1957), 298-299.

Review of poetry in three contemporary journals: *Western Review, Hudson Review, New World Writing.* "The Silent Generation is as good a name as any. It is a generation of poets who grew up amidst the intellectual wreckage of the century, between two battlefields, a generation deprived by their elders of every standard, every ideal except that of survival. Their sestinas, their Audenese, their footnoting do not promise much of a future for poetry or for anything else. They are all that is left of the Tradition in a time when the Tradition has become a symbol of bankruptcy."

C139   *Article:* "The First White Aboriginal," *Eigo Seinen (The Rising Generation),* CIII (November 1, 1957), 608-610; CIII (December 1, 1957), 669-671; CIV (February 1, 1958), 74-77; CIV (March 1, 1958), 133-136. Appears in English and Japanese, Reprinted, English only, in the *Walt Whitman Review,* V (September, 1959), 43-52.

"D.H. Lawrence has more in common with Walt Whitman than with any other man, and it was Lawrence who called Whitman the first white aboriginal.... Lawrence made a magnificent leap across civilization into the aboriginal darkness. He is one of the supreme heretics of white, modern civilization. And so for him to bless Walt with the title of the first white aboriginal is a matter of tremendous import.... Whitman did not have to spring; he sprouted, he vegetated, he loafed out of nowhere into the role of prophet and seer. At a single stroke, apparently without preparation, he became the one poet of America and Democracy. He is the one mystical writer of any consequence America has produced; the most original religious thinker we have; the poet of the greatest achievement; the first profound innovator; the most accomplished artist as well."

C140   *Article:* "The Unemployed Magician," *Poetry,* XCI (December, 1957), 194-209.

"Once in his life, at a time of his own choosing,
each poet is allowed to have an interview with
the god of letters. He is a real god, I think,
and maybe much more than that. He can answer all
questions about poetry.... The poet, unfortunately, cannot return with the answers; as he shakes
hands and says goodbye to the god, the visitor is
automatically brainwashed. All recollection of
the god's wisdom is obliterated and the poet returns home to write--criticism. Recently I held
my meeting with this deity.... Look at it this
way (he said). To the world you are a man set
apart because of your occupation, or rather vo-
cation, if you insist on calling it that. You
have a responsibility to maintain separateness.
It is a simple matter of distance by elevation.
Place any man on a stage, a platform or a soap-
box, and he is immediately transformed. The
angle of declension is what matters. But let
this man lose his distance and he is finished.
Among savages a magician who loses his hold over
the tribe is killed. So with you poets.... Now
if you will pardon this parlor trick, if you were
allowed to take one book of poems with you to a
desert island, which one would you take? Why,
I answered, I think I would take the poems of--
D. H. Lawrence."

1958

C141 *Poem:* "Western Town," *The New Yorker*, XXXIII
(February 15, 1958), 34.

C142 *Poem:* "Calling the Child," *The New Yorker*, XXXIV
(May 31, 1958), 34.

C143 *Review:* "The Auden Forgeries & the Pound Index,"
Prairie Schooner, XXXII (Spring, 1958), 73-75.

Review of *The Making of the Auden Canon*, by
Joseph Warren Beach ("At an advanced age Beach

felt it necessary to haul Auden into literary
court on the charge of forging his own poems.
The charge may not be unique in the annals of
poetry, but the evidence is unimpeachable....
Auden has suffered from adverse criticism more
than any poet in the twentieth century, not because he deserted Marx for the Church but because, as Isherwood once wrote, his character
changes with his hat. One wonders how so great
a talent could have given itself so completely
to time-serving and trickery"), and *Annotated
Index to the Cantos of Ezra Pound*, edited by
William W. Vaase ("Pound has been faithful to
his poetics from the beginning; his identity is
clear; his aims are known; and one can respect
him even as an enemy.... The work as a whole
provides one of the best tools for Pound scholarship as well as for modern poetry scholarship.
Its authors deserve commendations").

C144 *Article:* "Why Out-Russia Russia?" *The New Repub-
      lic*, CXXXVIII (June 9, 1958), 10-12.

"In recent months the world has witnessed a new
revolution—which I call the Russian Revolution
in American education.... Far from being a boon
to the humanities, the scientific competition
between Russia and America is liable to spell
the end of all humanistic culture throughout the
world.... Modern American literature—I mean
the real McCoy and not the bestseller list—is
not anti-American but anti-American-way-of-life.
There is a difference.... The abysmal failure
of technological civilization to provide man
with anything more than death and iceboxes has
spelled the end of scientific pre-eminence
throughout the world—everywhere except Russia,
the scientific seventh heaven. The question of
whether we are going to out-Russia Russia or
whether Russia is going to out-America America
is all one. Whatever is in store for us histor-
ically, it is our role as the guardians of man's
sensibilities to prevent as far as possible the

brutalization of our people by scientific hyster-
ia, by politics, and by promises of technological
rewards."

C145 *Letter:* "A Letter to American Poets and Libraries," *Poetry*, XCII (August, 1958), 330-331. Reprinted in *ALA Bulletin*, LII (September, 1958),
573-574.

"In the past few months I have received requests
from several of the great American libraries,
including the Library of Congress, to present
them with my manuscripts, letters, and similar
literary property.... The libraries of this
country are engaged in a competition to build up
manuscript collections of contemporary authors
without having to pay for them.... For American
libraries to speculate in the personal property
of authors seems completely out of character with
the aims and ideals of these great institutions.
I suggest to American poets that they refuse to
donate their manuscripts to libraries without
adequate payment."

C146 *Review:* "Aristotle Is a Skeleton," *Prairie
Schooner*, XXXII (Fall, 1958), 245-247.

Review of *Opus Posthumous*, by Wallace Stevens,
and *Wallace Stevens: An Approach to His Poetry
and His Thought* by Robert Pack. "Poetry to
Stevens was (to abbreviate) *in the absence of
God.* He began with this old Symbolist common-
place and ended with it. He tried to content
himself, as Mr. Pack rightly says, with being
the poet of the comic spirit, outside a tradition but within a genre. It is the genre of the
art of the earthly paradise in which the hero,
the romantic, the mystic are all indefinitely
and arbitrarily suspended from the premises.
He suffers from the congenital and evil dualism
of the modern intellectual who separates Art
and Life, Reality and Imagination, and who tries
to find a nexus through Philosophy.... At his

worst Stevens gives us the *chinoiserie* of modernism and at his best the problem itself. We will always read him for his dogged handling of the Problem."

C147   *Poem:* "Book Burial," *The New Republic*, CXXXIX (December 1, 1958), 18.

1959

C148   *Review:* "What is Irish Poetry," *Prairie Schooner*, XXXIII (Spring, 1959), 103-105.

Review of *The Oxford Book of Irish Verse* edited by Donagh MacDonaugh and Lennox Robinson. "The contemporary showing is very good, as good as the British themselves. Robert Graves, Louis MacNeice (one of the most under-rated twentieth century poets), and the later Day-Lewis, Padraic Fallon, Robert Farren, and of course Patrick Kavanaugh seem to have by-passed Yeats and are writing poems that bode well for the future. This is an honest, unpretentious, warm-hearted book, the rare kind of book one likes to carry around and not put on a shelf."

C149   *Article:* "Modern Poetry as a Religion," *American Scholar*, XXVIII (Summer, 1959), 297-305.

"The question is whether modern poetry has metamorphosed into a religion. And the answer is Yes. But then one must define both 'modern poetry' and 'religion,' a tedious business.... In the first place, modern poetry is not synonymous with contemporary poetry. Modern poetry, to my mind, refers to a group of writings of about one decade, say 1915-1925.... Not modern are D. H. Lawrence, William Carlos Williams, and Robert Frost.... Modern poetry is the official poetry of the twentieth century in all English-speaking countries. But properly speaking, it

is not a religion; *it is a surrogate for religion....* This religion has all the earmarks of
puritanism at its worst. Its bitterness, its
sense of exile from one or another homeland or
paradise, its strong theocratic flavor, its
sanctimoniousness, its hatred of spontaneity,
originality and freedom, its insistence on ortho-
doxy--these are all symptoms of the puritanical
hatred of poetry and its cynical abuse for the
purposes of power."

C150   *Article:* "The Critic in Spite of Himself," *Texas
Quarterly*, II (Autumn, 1959), 29-39.

"My criticism, and not my poetry, has carried me
around the world several times. I have lectured
on *Leaves of Grass* in Dublin and in Calcutta, on
William Carlos Williams in Hyderabad, on Edgar
Lee Masters in Salzburg, and on free verse in
Tokyo. As a critic I live in a Salvador Dali
universe. As a poet I live in Lincoln, Nebraska.
... The life of the critic has long since taken
the place of the life of the poet. There are no
Byrons in the twentieth century; only poor be-
deviled Dylan Thomases. Only him and the poet-
critics, as some cold-blooded lexicographer calls
us. I wonder if it has ever occurred to the poet
of our time that his audience prefers his criticism to his poetry because his poetry may be
lacking something? People, after all, are going
to have literature in some form, and if criticism
is all they can get, they will have criticism.
We hear of no critics in Shakespeare's day: maybe one or two, but nobody who would be invited
to address, say, a meeting of the National Council of the Teachers of English."

C151   *Review:* "Born of a Lifetime in New York," *The
New York Times Book Review* (October 4, 1959), 41.

Review of Marianne Moore's *O to Be a Dragon*.
"Modern criticism has held Marianne Moore in
such high esteem that one can hardly get to the

poems in her present volume for the glove-kiss-
ing gallantries on the dust-jacket.... In a
very real sense, Miss Moore is the creation of
T. S. Eliot and is his only American disciple.
Her poetry belongs to that decade of long ago
when Eliot and Pound captured poetry and criticism and turned them into a private enterprise
known as Modern Poetry. The slightly anachronistic quality of Miss Moore's poems is due to
the fact that she is still writing in the Twenties. So, for that matter, are Eliot and Pound."

C152   *Article:* "What's the Matter with Poetry," *The
New York Times Book Review* (December 13, 1959),
1, 22. Reprinted in *Nebraska Alumnus*, LVI
(March, 1960), 10-11, 29.

"Almost every art in the twentieth century is a
flourishing art--except poetry. Painting, music,
sculpture, architecture, even the novel and the
drama, have contributed richly to the age we
now live in. Our poetry, on the other hand, can
boast only a tangle of subtleties and grotesques
and the obscurantism for which it is famous. It
is a diseased art.... Ours is probably the only
poetry in history that has had to be *taught* in
its own time. A contemporary art that must be
taught to adults before it can be enjoyed is
sick.... Modern criticism is a propaganda for
a handful of power-hungry writers, many of whom
are the authors of the criticism itself.... T.
E. Hulme's book of criticism called *Speculations*
(1924) is something like the *Mein Kampf* of modern
criticism.... The 'poetry of ideas' is always a
third-rate poetry, and modern poetry is such."
According to the editor of *NYTBR*, "not for a long
time has the Book Review received such a flow of
mail." Thirty-five letters of response by other
writers to K.S. were printed in the January 10,
1960, issue of *NYTBR* under the title "Poetry
Today: The Reader and Mr. Shapiro."

1960

C153   *Letter:* "Voice of the Reader," *Chicago Sunday Tribune, Magazine of Books*, February 21, 1960.

A letter to the editor dealing with "vested interests of the new scholastic criticism" and "the literary smog."

C154   *Article:* "T.S. Eliot: The Death of Literary Judgement," *Saturday Review*, XLIII (February 27, 1960), 12-17, 34-36.

"The very idea of a summary of T.S. Eliot's writings seems a kind of blasphemy, or an act of unpardonable rudeness, for the Literary Situation (whatever that ecclesiastical expression is supposed to mean) is largely Eliot's invention, and for that reason it is all but imposible to discuss. Eliot is untouchable; he is Modern Literature incarnate and an institution unto himself. One is permitted to disagree with him on a point here or a doctrine there, but no more."

C155   *Article:* "The Jewish Writer in America," *American Judaism*, IX (Passover, 1960), 10-11, 22-27.

C156   *Article:* "PEN Meeting, Feb. 11, 1958," *The Eleusis of Chi Omega*, LXII (May, 1960), 246-254.

C157   *Article:* "Whitman Today," *Walt Whitman Review*, VI (June, 1960), 31-32.

A contribution to a Special Symposium Issue: Whitman, 1960. "It is wonderful to have lived through the drought of Modern Literature and to feel the healing influence of Whitman again.... One (like myself) who grew up in the waxworks of Modernism, among models of the Living, in a literary atmosphere where any breath of life or health was considered obscene, can hardly believe that the word 'Whitman' is again on every-

one's lips. It is a miracle, like spring in
winter. But that is what Whitman is for--these
miracles."

C158 *Review:* "A Non-New England Primer," *Prairie
Schooner*, XXXIV (Summer, 1960), 182-183.

Review of *The Henry Miller Reader*, edited by
Lawrence Durrell. "The probability of seeing
Miller whole today is quite remote: he is a great
dark continent thick with malaria, typhus, poi-
soned arrows, and venereal disease; and literary
science is just not ready for the safari....
This reviewer does not hesitate to name Miller
as the most vital literary critic of our time....
The plastic idols are brushed from their pedes-
tals almost unknowingly, *en passant*, throughout
his writings, and his real aim is to find the
living core of our world whenever it survives
and in whatever manifestation."

C159 *Poem:* "The Soldier," *Poetry London-New York*, I
(Summer, 1960), 44-45.

1961

C160 *Poems:* "A Garden in Chicago," "Emily Dickinson
and Katherine Anne Porter," "Surround," "A
Modest Funeral," "Waiting for the Pope," *Poetry,*
XCVIII (April, 1961), 1-6.

C161 *Letter:* "The Farmer and the Poet," *Poetry*, 98
(June, 1961), 170-185.

Response to Reed Whittemore's review of *In Defense of Ignorance* in this issue. "I am on the
side of the Ignoramuses, at least if we have to
make a choice between the connoisseur and the
Ignu--to use a Beatnik term.... When I teach
writing to young poets I start with this notion.
If they are to be poets, what they have to do

is to unwrap the layers of misinformation and
misconception in which they have been swaddled
since the day they were born. In order to be a
poet one must return to the state of poet, which
is a natural state of being, the childlike state
in which we see and sense everything in the full
light of consciousness and without having to
think our way to the truth. Thinking about art,
intellectualizing it, is the chief disease of
art in our day.... Poetry in America is un-
natural, artificial. The natural arts in this
country are the collective arts: jazz, films,
even TV. We are a primitive country, esthet-
ically speaking, and should probably remain so.
... There are broadly speaking only two possible versions of poetry: the biological view,
which I believe in, and the historical view....
The one is natural and uses nature as its standard; the other is artificial and uses history,
tradition, civilization, and the machine as its
standard."

C162 *Review:* "Voices That Speak to the Critic in Very
Different Rhythms," *The New York Times Book Review* (December 24, 1961), 4.

Review of Isabella Gardener's *The Looking Glass*,
Dilys Laing's *Poems from a Cage*, and May Sarton's
Cloud, Stone, Sun, Vine. Of *The Looking Glass*,
"It is an outstanding book. If I had anything
to do with it, I would nominate it for the Pulitzer Prize." "Dilys Laing's poems in her posthumous book are the works of a poet who has made
physical contact between herself and her craft.
Even her weaker poems are never faked and they
command respect." "It is pointless to be cruel
about bad poetry, but sometimes there is no
escape. Whatever May Sarton's other accomplish-
ments as a writer, she is a bad poet.... Her
poetry is lady-poetry at its worst--this at a
time when poetry is very much the art of women."

1962

C163   *Poem:* "Manhole Covers," *The New Yorker*, XXXVII (February 10, 1962), 36.

C164   *Poems:* "16 Poems" ["The world is my dream," "After a war the boys play soldier," "The two-year-old has had," "Land of my intellectual birth," "When the criminals cover their faces," "The landlord stands on a ladder," "August Saturday night on the Negro Street," "A communist artist was painting a pink pig," "From the top floor of the Tulsa hotel," "Next to my office where I edit my poem," "What the analyst said," "In the morning," "Each in her well-lighted picture-window," "They held a celebration for you, Charles," "The bourgeois poet closes the door of his study," "Condemned to write a long bad poem"], *College English* (May, 1962), 609-617.

C165   *Poems:* "Bad Taste, Inc.," "Human Nature," "You Call These Poems?" *Antioch Review*, XXII (Summer, 1962), 146.

C166   *Poems:* Selections from "The Bourgeois Poet," *Partisan Review*, XXIX (Summer, 1962), 406-415.

C167   *Poems:* Selections from "The Bourgeois Poet," *Poetry*, CI (October, 1962), 1-9.

C168   *Article:* "Rimbaud's Silence," *Prairie Schooner*, XXXIV (Summer, 1962), 145-148.

"*A Season in Hell* is without question the masterpiece of adolescence--the gangster age. There is probably nothing like it in any other literature.... Rimbaud the gangster poet and Rimbaud the engineer manqué are one and the same person. Both are children dreaming of their birthright. Both in a tantrum of cosmic proportions smash everything they can lay their hands on. Both are pre-Christian, pre-pagan, prior to Good and Evil--in a word, *modern*."

C169   *Article:* "The Three Hockey Games of T. S. Eliot,"
        The Antioch Review, XXII, 3 (Fall, 1962), 284-287.

        A response to Eliot's lecture in 1956 "to a
        Minneapolis multitude equalling that of three
        hockey games." "Eliot's triumph in the gymnas-
        ium proves nothing to me. (What an embarrass-
        ment it must have been to such a hater of audi-
        ences. One can imagine him trying to explain
        it away in his butler's English). The Minneap-
        olis mob scene, after all, consisted mostly of
        parochial students herded into buses by nuns,
        plus college students who are forced to cram
        Criticism, the New kind.... The sell-out of
        American poetry (no patriotism intended) result-
        ed in the kind of effeminate formalism which has
        been the fashion in this country for a generation
        and still is. The only healthy reaction against
        it is in the poems, lives, and acts of the var-
        ious 'disaffiliated' groups in the U.S. and
        around the world. Williams introduced *Howl*;
        that is a clue."

C170   *Review:* "Henry Miller: Important Reprints,"
        Prairie Schooner, XXXIV (Fall, 1962), 287-288.

        Review of Miller's *The Cosmological Eye, Sunday
        after the War,* and *Remember to Remember.* "New
        Directions has done more than any other publisher
        to put Henry Miller in the hands of American
        readers.... The three books form a kind of Mil-
        ler thesaurus or abstract of his life as a writer
        and man (with Miller, the two are one)." Also
        reviews *Henry Miller Between Heaven and Hell*,
        edited by Emil White. "This handsome paperback
        is a collection of essays, court opinions, dia-
        tribes, and what not, bearing upon the eternal
        Miller controversy.... Contains eighteen pages
        of photographs of Miller and his world, one of
        the best showing him exiting from a Paris *pis-
        soir*, looking very dapper."

1963

C171 *Poems:* Selections from "The Bourgeois Poet,"
      Kenyon Review, XXV (Spring, 1963), 344-347.

C172 *Article:* "Library, Asylum, Platform for Unin-
      hibited Leaps," *Wilson Library Bulletin*, 37, 8
      (April, 1963), 661-669.

      Address given in Baltimore, February 15, 1963,
      honoring Joseph L. Wheeler, librarian of the
      Pratt Library from 1926 to 1945. "It was under
      Joseph L. Wheeler that I began my career as a
      librarian. I had intended librarianship as my
      profession, and would perhaps be engaged in it
      today, except that the United States Army took
      me rather far afield." Much autobiographical
      information follows.

C173 *Poems:* Selections from "The Bourgeois Poet,"
      Shenandoah, 14, 4 (Summer, 1963), 42-46.

C174 *Poems:* "End Paper: Balcony Scene," "Vacation,"
      "Antipoem," "Death of a Student," "Basement
      Apartment," "Witches Are Flying," "Teamsters
      Union," *Poetry*, CIII (October, 1963), 90-96.

                        1964

C175 *Article:* "W. H. Auden's 'A Change of Air,'"
      Kenyon Review, XXVI (Winter, 1964), 196-199.

      A contribution to a symposium on Auden's "A
      Change of Air." "Nobody in his right mind is
      going to horse around with an Auden poem—even
      a blackboard poem like this one, written with
      one hand tied behind him. Talk about *an* Auden
      poem is anyhow irrelevant; he is a poet of
      issues and the issues are big. He is his own
      anthology, the typical poet of the age, the
      Explainer and all that.... A poet never con-

fuses his fame with the fame of his poems, it
seems to me. It is the others who do that (they
have no choice). Nothing is more remote from
the poet than what he has already published; I
daresay nothing is more painful to him than reading his old poems before an audience. Nothing
is more puzzling to him than those old poems.
Consequently he is the least equipped to say
what was intended."

C176 *Article:* "Is Poetry an American Art?" *College
English*, 25 (March, 1964), 395-405.

"American poetry nowadays has the reputation for
having accumulated a large and impressive body
of works. In the English language we are said
to be the present leader in the art. Numerically
as well as qualitatively, we make the best showing. Nevertheless, I believe that American poetry is a European transplantation which has
never really taken root with us and never will.
Ours is a hothouse poetry, kept alive by artificial respiration and fluorescent light. Otherwise, it is a poetry of brickbats.... We have
tried so hard--and failed--to produce a poetry
of sensibility. Let us give it up. We have
experimented with every extreme to no avail.
The art of poetry is foreign to us. To some
this is a bitter pill to swallow, but we'd
better take our medicine."

C177 *Poems:* "Abraham Lincoln," "Protestant," "Aunt
Lucy," "The Livingrooms of My Neighbors," *North
American Review*, N.S. I (March, 1964), 25-26.

C178 *Article:* "A Defense of Bad Poetry," *The Earlham
Journal* (Spring, 1964), 1-13.

"When a poet says he wants to write bad poems,
after he has succeeded in writing 'good' ones,
he is kicking over the traces. When he says
that change must come in content, he is asking
for a revolt against his own values not only in

literature but in everything else. He has come
to doubt the value of accepted literary 'contents'
and of his own psychic contents. He is in full
revolt; he is trying to break out. I too find
myself wanting to write Bad Poetry, poetry that
will not please, poetry that will subvert the
standards."

C179   *Article:* "What Is Creative Writing? or Playing
Footsie with the Philistines," *Descant,* VIII
(Summer, 1964), 2-18.

"Every person who has taught or engaged in a
Creative Writing Program has been aware of its
absurdity and its essential frivolousness. At
the same time, everyone is aware of the necessity
of the thing. I have seen terrible battles
fought between English Departments and Writing
Departments, battles in which the Trojan Horse
is usually destroyed. Nevertheless the writer
has become as familiar on the American campus as
the modernistic administration building."

C180   *Articles:* "A Malebolge of 1400 Books," *Carleton
Miscellany,* V, 3 (Summer, 1964), 3-135.

The entire issue is devoted to six lectures delivered by K.S. at Carleton College in April,
1964: "From Aristotle to Dante," "From Coleridge
to Eliot," "From Frost to Lawrence," "From Lau-
treamont to Robert W. Service," "From Shakespeare
to Yeats," "Henry Miller and Myself." "What better form of criticism can there be than a description of one's books, those basilisks that
sit year after year over a man's head and tell
him what he is. I thought of calling these lectures, 'Fourteen Hundred Books, a Personal Malebolge,' for after all, those books make a fine
torture chamber for any Inferno."

1965

C181 *Review:* "A Foot in the Door," *New York Herald Tribune, Book Week* (January 10, 1965), 3.

> A review of M.B. Tolson's *Harlem Gallery.* "A great poet has been living in our midst for decades and is almost totally unknown, even by the literati, even by the poets. Can this be possible in the age of criticism and of publication unlimited? It is not only possible, but highly probable. Poetry today is an established institution which has many of the characteristics of a closed corporation. (One of the rules of the poetic establishment is that Negroes are not admitted to the polite company of the anthology.) Poetry as we know it remains the most lily-white of the arts. A novelist and pamphleteer like Baldwin is world famous; M. B. Tolson, easily the literary equal of any number of Baldwins, is less honored in his own country than the most obscure poetaster."

C182 *Article:* "The Decolonization of American Literature," *Wilson Library Bulletin,* 39 (June, 1965), 843-853.

> "In every case except ours, a new culture is based on Home Country, Settler, and Native. But in America nobody knows where the Home Country is, for the Settlers come from Home Countries all over the world; and the Natives are no more. We have no Natives and no common Home Country. We have no peasantry. We have only expatriates and ex-slaves. This is a country of Runaways and Captives.... The great theme of American literature is rootlessness.... Insofar as the American writer is true to his situation, he is a neurotic, ridden with the anxieties of separateness from the past. Freedom is one of the beneficent symptoms of this anxiety. We are suddenly confronted with an alphabet of freedoms ranging from civil rights to freedom of the

banned book and the spoken obscenity. Our literature is engaging in a Socratic dialogue with all
previous values; we do this with increasing reck-
lessness and frequently with cynicism, for what
is there to lose? The fact is, there is no place
to go back to; we have nowhere to go but forward.
We cannot help ourselves; that is our condition."

1966

C183   *Review:* "Classicists All," *The New York Times
Book Review* (January 9, 1966), 12.

Review of William Faulkner's *The Marble Faun and
A Green Bough, Poems, 1922-1961* by Donald Davidson, *Collected Poems of Rolfe Humphries*, and
Louis Simpson's *Selected Poems.* "With Faulkner,
the incredible mediocrity of the poetry becomes
a major question, for not all great writers of
fiction have been such miserable poets.... Davidson is Neo, below-the-Mason-and-Dixon classical,
influenced more by Robert Frost and Confederate
corn than the real thing. Yet he writes what he
must and how he must, and well.... Simpson is
modern, angry, saturnine champing at the bit and
biting his fingernails. He is interesting."

C184   *Poem:* "Americans Are Afraid of Lizards," *Poetry*,
CX (April, 1966), 3.

C185   *Review:* "The Charmed Circle of Anais Nin," *Chicago Sun-Times, Book Week* (May 1, 1966), 3.

"For a generation the literary world on both
sides of the Atlantic has lived with the rumor
of an extraordinary diary. Early readers of the
manuscript discussed it in breathtaking superla-
tives as a work that would take its place with
the great revelations of literature. A significant section of this diary is at last in print
and it appears that the great claims made for it

are justified.... For lack of terminology, this
Diary is what the University of Chicago would
call a great book. It is great because of its
inherent qualities of style, perspicuity, and
natural organization, but more because it is
unclassifiable as a book at all. If it is a
book it is a new and beautiful kind, shining a
strange light on literature itself."

C186 *Article:* "To Have Been a Poet," *Prospect* (May,
      1966), 34-47.

C187 *Poem:* "There was that Roman poet who fell in love
      at fifty-odd," *Steppenwolf* (Winter, 1966), 14.

C188 *Article:* "A Jew Looks at Atheism," *American
      Judaism* (Winter, 1966), 7, 28-29.

      "It is astounding that intellectuals still con-
      fuse religion and God-consciousness. Atheists
      are usually conspicuous for two qualities among
      others: the absence of the sense of humor and
      the presence of a hydrocephalic historical con-
      sciousness. Atheists have history on the brain,
      like a form of housemaid's knee.... The Jew is
      the criterion of God-consciousness in America....
      In order for a Jew to desert, he has to cover his
      tracks so completely that he must be a kind of
      madman and make a career of hiding his identity.
      What I am saying is that *Jewish Atheist* is a con-
      tradiction in terms. *Jew* means *in the presence
      of God* by definition. Whether the Jew acknowl-
      edges the presence or shrugs it off is his bus-
      iness."

C189 *Poem:* "How Do You Walk?" *Saturday Evening Post*,
      239 (December 31, 1966), 42.

                         1967

C190 *Review:* "The Sorrows of Dahlberg," *Chicago Sun-*

Times, Book Week (February 5, 1967), 5, 12.

Review of *Epitaphs of Our Times: The Letters of Edward Dahlberg.* "Under the garbled and crabbed rhetoric his cries are the common cries for money and respect from those he has affronted. One must admire his desperation to publish these letters which, far from adding to his name, can only muddy it. Writers who use the mails for posterity almost always come a cropper. Great letters are written to the recipient, not to the world. All the same, this collection of letters adds another document to the long Napoleonic retreat of the artist; it is one more testimonial of defeat."

C191 *Review:* "Our heroes off their horses," *Chicago Sun-Times, Book Week* (February 26, 1967), 17-18.

Review of New Directions reprint of *In the American Grain*, by William Carlos Williams. "It is one of the dead-center bombdrops on the American soul by the most American American since Whitman. It exposes with love and horror America 'perversely flowering....' Williams' mystique of the Local defined his Americanness. During the Twenties he tried to placate the anti-American fury and the expatriates by his negative defenses of the primary American heroes and villains. To desert America in the flesh seemed to Williams a capital crime: one must stay on the frontier (in Williams' case, New Jersey) and battle the spirit of place. The poet must, with certain knowledge of defeat, stand his ground on the terrain more hostile to poetry than any locale ever known or imagined. There is this element of heroism in Williams, the cunning of Odysseus, the shrillness of the outraged sensibility, the demand for the truth, the pounding on the table, the bleeding prose."

C192 *Review:* "Shelley Unseen," *Chicago Sun-Times, Book Week* (March 5, 1967), 14.

Review of *The Mutiny Within* by James Rieger.
"This book cannot have been anything but a Ph.D.
thesis. If so, it is not even a brilliant Ph.D.
thesis. The writing, far from beautiful, is
graceless, brutally pedantic, arrogantly super-
ior, and hysterical. The patois of the doctoral
candidate gets in the way of the discussion of
material so dense to begin with that one ends
with a rigmarole. Books dealing with the her-
metic and occult aspects of poetry should at
least *strive* for clarification; this one seems
to strive for deeper darkness."

C193   *Review:* "The Poet as Hero," *Chicago Daily News,
       Panorama* (March 18, 1967), 7.

Review of two books by Keith Douglas, *Alamein to
Zem Zem* and *Collected Poems*. "Keith Douglas
was killed at the age of 24 in the Normandy in-
vasion, after gathering information from behind
enemy lines. Like so many British poets his
bravery was extraordinary. (American soldier-
poets are never cited for heroism. The British
soldier-poet, especially of the officer class,
leaps into battle joyously and brilliantly)....
Douglas died too young to become the poet he had
in him. He is no Wilfred Owen, nor even a Sassoon, certainly no Dylan Thomas. He was a poet
marked with the talons of the Muse, nevertheless,
playing with Her, wooing, retreating, laughing
even in the face of death."

C194   *Review:* "The Poet's Joy," *The New York Times
       Book Review* (May 7, 1967), 8.

Review of *Northfield Poems* by A.R. Ammons, and
Half Sun Half Sleep by May Swenson. "The poet's
joy is in the writing. When the writing is joy-
ous enough it carries over to the reader and becomes contagious, like laughter. Mr. Ammons'
poems in his new book are joyless and depress-
ing.... Unable, apparently, to face the joy of
language, he can only parry it and assert his

indifference. Talented or not, he sends a cold
shiver through the reader. In high contrast,
May Swenson leaps to the love of language and
has a ball. It hardly matters what her subject
is. Her concentration on the verbal equivalent
of experience is so true, so often brilliant,
that one watches her with hope and pleasure,
praying for victory all the way."

C195   *Review:* "The Novel of Her Life," *Chicago Sun-
Times, Book Week* (June 18, 1967), 4, 12.

Review of *The Diary of Anais Nin, Volume II.*
"The first public release of the Anais Nin
Diary covered the years 1930-1934 and is a por-
tion of the immense journal begun in childhood.
The second volume covers the years 1934-1939.
The two volumes span what is probably the crucial decade of the 20th century, the decade that
poets, intellectuals, and historians will never
cease to debate. The interior dialogue of Anais
Nin throws an enduring indirect light on those
terrible ten years. It is the last time that
the artist can pretend to be free.... The extraordinary fact about the members of the Nin 'group'
is the persistence of their disengagement. It
is also their primary message. Almost all the
major characters of the diary are examples of the
modern artist driven to the depths of the psyche."

C196   *Article:* "Class of '67: The Gentle Desperadoes,"
The Nation, 204 (June 19, 1967), 776-777.

Part of a symposium on college education c. 1967.
"Since World War II college students and their
juniors have lived in a climate of absolute con-
tempt, a climate created and fostered by their
parents and their institutions. Crude and hypo-
critical government actions abroad and at home
have re-inforced the belief of the new genera-
tions that everything is SHIT. The most common
noun, adjective, verb and mark of punctuation in
their language is SHIT. No poem dares to leave

the word out. No painting. No simile. The
motto of the new generation of the Left might be:
Blood, Nirvana, Shit."

C197 *Review:* "The Wicked Scientist," *The New York
Times Book Review* (August 6, 1967), 8.

Review of *Herakles, A Play in Verse*, by Archibald
MacLeish, and *New and Selected Poems: 1932-1967*
by Peter Viereck. "In a time when kindergarten
drama such as *MacBird* is acclaimed by the organ-
ized 'avant-garde,' a play such as *Herakles* will
probably be passed over or damned with faint
praise. That would be a pity; MacLeish's new
play is as virile and as stageworthy as *J.B.*,
which is saying a good deal.... Viereck's collection of poems covers the period of the crucial
generation (from the Depression to today) which
one sometimes fears is the Last Generation. Collected volumes are always full of unfulfilled
wishes, but poets dream of being judged by their
best. Viereck is a well-known professor of history and a professional political theorist of
repute. The spill-over of his *metier* as histor-
ian into his poetry is unfortunate. There is
endless ranting, mostly in quaint, disqualified
meters, nearly all on the socio-political plane."

C198 *Poems:* "Five Poems," *The New Yorker*, 43 (August
12, 1967), 38.

C199 *Review:* "The Cutting Edge," *Chicago Sun-Times,
Book Week* (September 24, 1967), 14.

Review of *Of Flesh and Bone* by John Frederick
Nims ("John Nims is learned, but a poet"); *Sixty
Poems of Martial in Translation* by Dudley Fitts
("Fitts is learned, but not a poet. In trans-
lating or paraphrasing sixty of the short poems
of Martial he fails to convey either the cutting
elegance of the Latin or the brutal wit with
which the Roman impaled his contemporaries");
Poems Written in Early Youth by T. S. Eliot

("Eliot buffs will not rejoice in the publication
of his juvenilia, but term papers will abound");
In Glad Thanksgiving by John Masefield ("Masefield belongs to that last phase of English before America ruled out meters.... One reads the
volume with a sigh, or perhaps a sigh of relief");
Mark Van Doren: 100 Poems ("One of the great
teachers of our time and perhaps one of the last
lovers of literature for its own sake, Van Doren
writes every poem with love"); *The Marches* by
James Scully, and *Voyages Down and Other Poems*
by Charles Philbrick ("The writing is unmistak-
ably skilled and, within limits, inventive. Nothing, in fact, is missing except the primary emo-
tions: rage, ecstacy, terror"); *The Rose of Soli-
tude* by Brother Antoninus ("A kind of versified
put-on with a high volume of theological static
and a still higher volume of caterwauling. At
best the book is a minor obscenity"); *The Poems
of Doctor Zhivago* by Boris Pasternak ("The translator has taken liberties not so much with meaning as with tone, and has managed to reduce these
powerful poems to bathos").

C200 *Review:* "Pop, Kid Stuff, & Poetry," *Chicago Sun-
Times, Book Week* (October 8, 1967), 12.

Review of *Pop Poems* by Ronald Gross ("What at
first glance seems inane and childish tinkering
with words develops into startling poem-like
structures. One is made to see a different
dimension of even the meanest language"); *An
Alphabestiary* by John Ciardi ("Ciardi has the
unpleasant mannerisms of pointing his finger at
you and telling you to sit down.... One thinks
of D.H. Lawrence and wishes for that influence
to return"); *Sister My Life* by Boris Pasternak
("It is as poet that Pasternak reaches his high-
est achievement").

C201 *Review:* "The Poetry of Spilled Blood," *Chicago
Tribune, Book World* (October 8, 1967), 4.

Review of *O the Chimneys* by Nelly Sachs. "Nelly
Sachs' poetry is written in German, the language
that Hitler took away from the Jews. Her German
is printed opposite the English translation, as
if with a jeer, for these are the poems that won
the Nobel Prize in 1966. The poetry is absolute
lament.... All her poems are one poem, as it
were, maintaining the level of sublimity of the
Biblical lamentations. The poetry therefore belongs more to scripture than to literature."

C202 *Poems:* "From White-Haired Lover," *Poetry,* CXI
(October, 1967), 1-4.

C203 *Review:* "A Nervous Naked Sword on Naked Feet,"
Chicago Sun-Times, Book Week (November 19, 1967),
3.

Review of *The Complete Poems of Marianne Moore.*
"Marianne Moore is more adored than read, more
esteemed than appreciated, more coddled than
understood. T. S. Eliot knighted her as the
grand dame of modern poetry in 1935 and she has
lived the part to a T, as elegant and brittle as
a Sitwell. Time has not tampered with her wits
or with her reputation and she remains one of
the aristocrats of the Modern.... Her poetry is
decorative in the extreme, arid and rich at the
same time, like the fringe of an oasis."

C204 *Review:* "Showdown at City of Poetry," *Chicago
Sun-Times, Book Week* (December 3, 1967), 5.

Review of *The Poetry Circus* by Stanton A.
Coblentz ("Approximately annually, the last
literary philistine in captivity comes clanking
down the hall on his donkey to shoot up the City
of Poetry.... Wearing the button that says 'Down
With the Nonpoets and the Antipoets,' he charges
into Modern Poetry firing pointblank at everybody in any anthology printed after 1910, spar-
ing only Robert Frost, E.A. Robinson and one or
two ladies. In the sunset, after this quixotic

figure has departed, all the poets search his
published report to see if they have been listed
among the clobbered--and breathe a sigh of relief to find that they are"); *The Blue Swallows*
by Howard Nemerov ("Nemerov is one of the exquis-
ite stylists of the neo-Modern.... Mercilessly
well-behaved, he gives the lie to the salesman
from Philistina concerning the manners of the
modern poet"); *Selected Poems 1938-1958* by Delmore Schwartz ("Like so many contemporary artists
and poets, Schwartz made a career of alienation
and would not permit himself the luxury and
slight protection of wit.... His poetry is dark
and crude but crawling with force, like pinch-
blende. It is unlikely that it will be forgot-
ten"); *Short Poems* by John Berryman ("John Berryman is an up-and-coming name.... Photogenic,
newsworthy, rococo and ambitious, he has the
literary critics eating out of his hand"); *Collected Shorter Poems 1927-1957* by W. H. Auden
("It is a solid achievement in every way....
Among the foremost poets writing in the English
language in our century Auden alone has main-
tained civilized relations with the community at
large. In a sense, it is his mission").

1968

C205 *Review:* "The Failure of Dissidence," *Chicago
Sun-Times, Book Week* (February 4, 1968), 7.

Review of *Hawkweed* by Paul Goodman ("Random
House has published a new collection of Paul
Goodman's poems; why, this reviewer is attempt-
ing to fathom. Goodman is a writer of rich and
exhibitionistic personality, disarmingly charming in his constant protests of failure, failure
as an artist, failure as a man"); and *The Liver-
pool Scene*, edited by Edward Lucie-Smith ("In
the dozen or so years since the Movement began
its hard sell it has been able to market only

snake oil and dowsing wands, children's records
and Coonskin.... Their poetry has sunk to a
low which even the most gifted enemies of the
Movement could not foresee").

C206   *Review:* "Three 'Xrist' Poets," *Chicago Sun-Times,
        Book Week* (March 10, 1968), 10.

Review of *The Back Country* by Gary Snyder ("Snyder is one of the two or three Beat poets whose
work survived the crude and brutal poetics of
his Bay Area confreres.... But the goal of his
pilgrimage, whatever it is, lies far in the distance"); *Visions of Christ* by Rainer Maria Rilke
("Although the poems were written in his early
twenties, Rilke could never bring himself to
publish them, partly out of fear of his mother's
Roman Catholic orthodoxy, and partly because he
regarded them as too much a part of the intimate
recesses of his mind"); *The Poems of Saint John
of the Cross*, revised and rewritten by John Frederick Nims, Preface by Robert Graves ("For more
than a decade John Frederick Nims has put his
gifts as a poet and translator at the service
of the divine love poet, St. John of the Cross.
His new English versions of the 16th Century
Spanish poet will in all probability remain the
definitive English translations.... As a preface, Robert Graves has contributed a wild and
whirling essay in which he elevates the Spanish
ecstatic poet to the status of a Muse poet.
Sweeping through history and prehistory like a
warlock, Graves rescues him in proximity to the
company of the near-erotic and the orgiastic
poets of the pre-Christian ages").

C207   *Article:* "To Abolish Children," *Esquire*, LXIX
        (April, 1968), 119-121.

"Throughout human history the fine arts have
provided the nexus between intuitional insight
and civilized hindsight. That is what the arts
have been for. But at times when intuition

usurps the more wakeful states of mind, the arts
plunge into the playpen and the cry of 'immediacy'
fills the air. Immediacy (as in D.H. Lawrence's
'immediate present' or the Zen Now!) cripples
hindsight and deliberation and prevents criteria
from coming into existence. The failure of the
Beat community to create poetry or any of the
other arts is the most significant fact about
the Movement. The hidden aesthetic premise of
the Movement is that art is evil and must be
hamstrung. Only states of consciousness are
valid: drug-states, violence in bed and on the
street, secret languages, political nihilism.
These are the lingua franca of the Movement."

C208 *Poem:* "Man on Wheels," *Mademoiselle*, 67 (May,
1968), 140.

C209 *Review:* "Mangling a Masterpiece," *Chicago Sun-
Times, Book Week* (May 19, 1968), 3.

Review of *The Original Rubaiyyat of Omar Khayaam*,
translated by Robert Graves and Omar Ali-Shah.
"Robert Graves is a restorer, but how good a one
is highly debatable.... What is the meaning of
this anachronistic campaign against the old Vic-
torian chestnut? Is it part of Graves' charming
and kooky revival of the Muse as whirling dervish?
Or is there a more general significance to this
minor act of vandalism? Two answers: Graves'
lifelong repudiation of 'rational' and 'official'
poetry and his own failure as a modern poet."

C210 *Poem:* "Epithalamium, the second time around,"
Northwest Review, 10 (Summer, 1968), 65-66.

C211 *Poems:* "Manhole Covers," "Bad Taste, Inc.," "Man
on Wheels," "Hollywood," "Auto Wreck," "A Calder,"
"The Conscientious Objector," "Calling the Child,"
Literary Cavalcade (Teacher's Edition) (November,
1968), 13-15.

C212 *Interview:* "Poets, Society, and Religion," *The
Lutheran Witness* (November, 1968), 20-22.

With Mark Van Doren, W.D. Snodgrass, Conrad
Aiken, Allen Ginsberg, Richard Eberhart, Thom
Gunn, and John Ciardi, K.S. answers questions
posed by Jack Ledbetter concerning religion,
God, and poetry. Q: "In your opinion why are
there so few religious poets today?" A: "Seriously, I thought there were many. Not only
the Audens and the Mertons but all those cruddy
oriental-style mystics."

C213   *Review:* "An Amiable, Decent, Law-Abiding Non-
       Poet," *Chicago Tribune, Book World* (November 24,
       1968), 4.

       Review of *Lonesome Cities* by Rod McKuen. "Now
       Random House has published four books by Rod Mc-
       Kuen, a lower-middlebrow crooner who has sold
       more than fifty million records of his croons,
       which are also his poems.... It is irrelevant
       to speak of McKuen as a poet. His poetry is
       not even trash."

C214   *Poems:* "Good Friday Music," "Reeking With Love,"
       "July the Fourth," *Tri Quarterly*, 11 (Winter,
       1968), 182, 191, 196.

1969

C215   *Review:* "Major Poets of the Ex-English Language,"
       Chicago Tribune, Book World (January 26, 1969), 4.

       Review of *The Complete Poems* by Randall Jarrell,
       and *His Toy, His Dream, His Rest: 308 Dream Songs*
       by John Berryman. "At the moment, when twentieth-
       century poetry has taken on the odor and aspect
       of a hog wallow, let us look at two actual poets.
       Randall Jarrell's poetry ... is a body of work
       which is already permanent and will serve as a
       standard of achievement for a long time to come.
       ... John Berryman and Jarrell were friends,
       associates and collaborators in the Sisyphean
       effort to write poetry in American. Since Jar-

rell's death in 1965 Berryman has surpassed his
own brilliant and famed *77 Dream Songs*. The 77
poems now total 385 and comprise a major poetic
work of our time and place."

C216 *Review:* "Hair Stylist of a Generation," *Chicago
Tribune, Book World* (May 25, 1969), 6.

Review of *Allen Ginsberg in America* by Jane Kra-
mer, and *Ankor Wat* by Allen Ginsberg. "One
should not take Ginsberg or his printed work
seriously, but only their consequences. He is
the hair stylist of a generation; a poor poet
who never learned the trade; a weak thinker who
settles most questions with a homemade brand of
mushy-minded Hinduism, a deacon in the crusade
for drugs, a minor Marxist scoutmaster leading
his rabble to the fountain of youth."

C217 *Review:* "The Poet as Early 20th Century Bohemian,"
Chicago Tribune, Book World (July 6, 1969), 4.

Review of *Selected Letters of E.E. Cummings.*
"This collection of letters, which spans the life
of Cummings the poet and Cummings the man, will
not add to the stature of the poet or of the man.
Nevertheless, as letters are bound to do, they
provide us with a characterization of the man behind the artist. For better or for worse, the
door opens upon a poet answering his mail--in
this case a dedicated and beloved poet moseying
through life.... The letters seem the detritus
of a fine, controlled and delicate talent. They
reflect the poet off duty and cannot be expected
to measure up to his art. Unfortunately they do
reflect the art, forcing us to look at the poems
again with a colder eye and a slightly raised
eyebrow."

C218 *Poem:* "Moving In," *Poetry,* CXV (November, 1969),
123-126.

1970

C219 *Article:* "The Poetry Wreck," *Library Journal*, 95
(February 15, 1970), 623-635.

Adapted from a speech delivered to a pre-confer-
ence session of the California Library Association in San Francisco, December 8, 1970. "At
the center of all human culture stands the library. At the center of civilization stands the
library. But now and then the apocalyptic question crosses our minds: Is the library still
standing? If the university is moving toward a
new Dark Age, what of the library? If standards
of value in every department of modern life are
being threatened by barbarism and savagery, what
of the books themselves and their keepers? I am
no Jeremiah and will leave the ranting to others.
But as a teacher of reading and writing, as a
reader and writer myself, as a literary critic
and professor of literature for some 20 years,
as a functionary of the teaching world, a proud
member of the Establishment and what one poet
calls a shameless patriot, I wish to report to
you my version of the degeneration of the literary intelligence and its attendant confusions
everywhere in our lives."

Note: According to a note by K.S. in *An Annual
Supplement to Bio-Bibliography* (July 1, 1968-
June 1, 1970), "This item was reprinted in part
or as a whole in other magazines and possibly
more than a hundred newspapers, and was the subject of a radio talk and NBC interview. There
is no way to trace the names of the reprinters;
I am in contact with the Author's Guild concerning copyrights."

C220 *Poem:* "Aubade," *The Quarterly Journal of the
Library of Congress* (April, 1970), 142-143.

C221 *Poems:* "The Race," "Joe and Gene," "University
Revisited," "There Are No Ghettos," "People's

Park," "Hair," "The Peace Sign," "Stop the Dia-
logue," "Rock Festival," "The Radical Rich,"
"Isms," "Sociology," "The Students with the
Turned Down Mouths," "Sestina: of the Militant
Vocabulary" [with prose introduction], *Esquire*,
LXXIII (May, 1970), 131-134.

C222 *Review:* "Through Labyrinth of Huxley's Mind,"
Los Angeles Times, Calendar (July 12, 1970), 50,
53.

Review of *Letters of Aldous Huxley*, edited by
Grover Smith. "Very often the letters of a famous writer can compromise his reputation: and
although this is not the case with Aldous Huxley,
his correspondence does provide the necessary
commentary on his life.... Had Huxley devoted
his talents to the eradication of this symptom
of sociopathology (Dadaism) rather than swooning
into mushrooms and the One, he would have done a
service to modern culture for which the world
would thank him. Unfortunately, his life tra-
jectory is one of slow and gentlemanly retreat,
a bowing out--backwards, into the Oriental soup."

C223 *Article:* [tribute to Edward Dahlberg] *Tri Quarterly*, 19 (Fall, 1970), 123-124.

                              1971

C224 *Review:* "Passport Carrying Member of the Academy,"
Los Angeles Times Book Review (January 24, 1971),
10, 12.

Review of Kenneth Rexroth's *With Eye & Ear*. "The
San Francisco happening was a birth, surely, but
more in the nature of the hippo-griff than of the
messiah. It appears by general consent that the
happening is now over, and rumor has it that Rexroth is now a member of the academy, with passport.... Rexroth is a stylist of the genus aris-

tocrat revolte; cheapness and vulgarity appall
him. He is the most learned and wide-ranging of
all the adversary poets of our time; he is con-
versant with the originals of the many languages
he translates, and he is well-versed in the
Eastern mystical and metaphysical writers. But
all his opinions--and he is as opinionated as
H. L. Mencken--are rooted in the dogmas and plat-
itudes of historical and social overthrow....
These essays are almost entirely book reviews.
Rexroth has reinstated the book review as a serious form of criticism."

C225 *Poem:* "My Lesbia," *Concerning Poetry* (Spring,
1971), 12.

C226 *Poem:* "Catullus 101," *California Quarterly*, I
(Spring, 1971), 1.

C227 *Review:* "'Avantgarde': Prayer for a New Alienation," *Los Angeles Times Book Review* (April 25,
1971), 1, 6.

Review of *The Perennial Avantgarde* by Gerald
Sykes. "Sykes is a neophiliac. A neophiliac is
a worshipper of the new.... Books on Culture
Crash are now proliferating, as this one attests.
Our author uses the sack of Columbia University
as a kind of off-stage background for his monologue.... What we have here is an activist-in-
tellectual bible, a manual of sensibility train-
ing, or a spockistic handbook on the care and
feeding of values. The center of value, to be
sure, is the student, holiest of creatures....
If, somewhere, there is an antonym to the word
Renaissance, this book would be an example of it."

1972

C228 *Review:* "Scraping the Bottom of the Roethke
Barrel," *New Republic*, 166 (March 4, 1972), 24.

Review of *Straw for the Fire: From the Notebooks of Theodore Roethke, 1943-1963*, edited and arranged by David Wagoner. "Roethke was fortunate in publication and could have no complaint about his eventual recognition as poet. He swept the board of literary honors and even had his eye on 'the Swedish prize.' In this he was presumptuous, for he was a poet of conscious limitations and slight range, though one whose limitations shielded him from cant and spared him wasteful effort. His strength was narrowness. He pumped his sensibility through narrow pipes and built up a considerable head of steam. He kept his hand upon the throttle of the poem and his eye upon the rail of recognition. He was a success, perhaps even a cultural hero. Roethke, like most good poets, was his own best critic: one doubts that he would have loosed these papers on the public."

C229   *Poem:* "Girls Working in Banks," *Esquire*, LXXVII (June, 1972), 193.

C230   *Poem:* "Flying First Class," *New Republic*, 167 (August, 1972), 30.

1973

C231   *Poems:* "The Garage Fool," "Moon Walk," "Garage Sale," "A Curiosity," *Audience* (January-February, 1973).

C232   *Poem:* "Parliament of Poets," *New Republic*, 168 (February 24, 1973), 31.

C233   *Review:* "The new poetry: still echoing the agony of the '60s," *Chicago Tribune, Book World* (March 25, 1973), 1.

Review of *The Living Mirror: Five Young Poets from Leningrad*, edited by Suzanne Massie ("Care-

fully and lovingly introduced by their editor");
Poems of Mao Tse-tung ("Most of these poems would
be meaningless without the running commentary of
the editors"); *Ain't No Ambulances for No Nigguhs
Tonight* by Stanley Crouch ("Almost as anachronistic as *Uncle Tom's Cabin*"); *Debridement* by
Michael Harper ("Sticks with the symbolism of
guns, sex, and the slave ship"); *Revolutionary
Petunias* by Alice Walker ("Human and personal,
not written as illustrations of an abstract dialectic"); *Winning Hearts and Minds: War Poems by
Vietnam Veterans* ("An openly agit-prop end-the-
war document and unlike most of the war poetry
written at home has the ring of truth"); *A Day
Book* by Robert Creeley ("The poetry section perpetuates the technique of the Pound-Williams-
Black Mountain style"); *Sleepers Joining Hands*
by Robert Bly ("Bly praises the resurgence of
matriarchy and states that 'praise of the fem-
inine soul' is his theme"); and Robin Morgan's
Monster ("Morgan's message, as she emphasizes
in her poetry, is political, the attempt to
vilify, modify, and eventually overthrow the
masculine culture which enslaves women"). The
article concludes that "nearly all the poets
mentioned above operate from a single set of
stock political responses. By a process of the
misappropriation of values they proclaim themselves to be the rightful heirs of poetry and
of society. And this they are not."

C234 *Poem:* "Crossing Lincoln Park," *Chicago Tribune,
Magazine* (May 20, 1973), 80.

C235 *Poem:* "Jefferson's Greeting," *Esquire*, LXXIX
(May, 1973), 68.

C236 *Poem:* "The Heiligenstadt Testament (Beethoven
Dying)," *The New York Quarterly*, 14 (Spring,
1973), 73-74.

C237 *Review:* "The Poetry of Bob Dylan," *The New Republic*, 168 (June 2, 1973), 28.

Review of *Writings and Drawings* by Bob Dylan. "This stunning book is practically a full quarto --not quite 9 1/2 by 12 inches, but so proportioned. The cover is a brilliant water-proof magenta with a full-sized photograph of the poet on the back cover.... One can only commend the publisher for this extraordinary display of confidence in poetry. And with the word 'poems' so wisely in small italics."

C238   *Poem:* "The Piano Tuner's Wife," *Kayak*, 32 (1973), 9.

C239   *Review:* "The sad (but hardly sudden) decline of English poetry," *Chicago Tribune, Book World* (June 3, 1973), 3.

Review of *The New Oxford Book of English Verse 1250-1950*, edited by Helen Gardner, and *The Oxford Book of 20th Century English Verse*, edited by Philip Larkin. "Helen Gardner is a 20th century mind and soul, one of the best scholars of the metaphysical and modern poets we have.... Where Helen Gardner leaves off, Philip Larkin picks up, and the going is hard. *The Oxford Book of 20th Century English Verse* is a virtual confession of the bankruptcy of English poetry in England.... Compare any American anthology of the 20th century ... and one will wince."

1974

C240   *Poem:* "Philomela, Procne, Terus," *Poetry*, CXXIII (March, 1974), 319-323.

C241   *Poem:* "The Humanities Building," *The New Yorker*, 50 (May 13, 1974), 40.

1975

C242 *Poem:* "The Minute," *The Nation*, 220 (February 24, 1975).

C243 *Poem:* "Auden," *Harvard Advocate* (April, 1975).

C244 *Article:* "The Writer's Sense of Place," *South Dakota Review*, 13, 3 (Autumn, 1975), 68.

Short contribution to a symposium. "For all its guff, William Carlos Williams' dogma of the Local remains the touchstone of what authentic American poetry we have. Whitman tried the Local on the heroic scale, mapping the continent. Nothing very local there but at least he dared the idiom to come into being. And despite the adversary esthetic of the Modern, the programmatists, the pseudo-revolutionaries, the doom-sayers, the boors of protest and cant, an idiom, a language, emerges." Abstracted from introduction by K.S. to Ted Kooser's *A Local Habitation & a Name*.

C245 *Poem:* "Adult Bookstore," *Poetry Now*, II (April, 1975), 4.

C246 *Poems:* "The Martini," "My Fame's Not Feeling Well," *Poetry Now*, II (September, 1975), 2. [Note: also includes an article on K.S. by William Childress based on an extensive interview with the poet].

C247 *Poem:* "White Negress (Brancusi-Chicago Art Institute)," *Esquire*, LXXXIV (December, 1975), 186.

1976

C248 *Article:* "The American-Jewish-Writer," *Melus*, III (Summer, 1976), 6-9.

Part of a "Special Number: The Contemporary

Writer and His Sense of Ethnicity." "I thought
of changing my name in order to get my poems
published. I must have been nineteen. I had
never read a poem by a Jewish-name poet except
one, a James Oppenheimer. I wrote him; I don't
remember any reply. Shortly after I discovered
the *Partisan Review* with Delmore Schwartz and
Philip Rahv and those Jewish-sounding names.
When that magazine began to publish me I felt
that I had found a home, even ideologically....
I would say that the American-Jewish writer is
condemned to comedy. There is no great poetry
by American Jews or Americans about the Nazi
holocaust."

1977

C249 *Review:* "Flirting with madness and death," *Chicago Tribune, Book World* (October 23, 1977), 1,
9.

Review of *Anne Sexton: A Self-Portrait in Letters*,
edited by Linda Gray Sexton and Louis Ames.
"These letters contribute to the building of
Anne Sexton's monument. The motive therefore
is honorable. Nevertheless the nagging question
remains: would the poet have wanted to make these
letters public?... Any glorification of suicide,
however unintentional, is pernicious. The maimed
poet is never at the center of great art."

D. ANTHOLOGIES

D1 *An American Anthology.* Tom Boggs, ed. Prairie
    City, Ill.: Decker, 1942. *Contains:* "Necropolis,"
    "Buick," The Confirmation."

D2 *Anthology of Magazine Verse for 1938-1942, and
    Yearbook of American Poetry.* Alan F. Pater, ed.
    New York: The Paebar Company, 1942. *Contains:*
    "October 1."

D3 *American Harvest.* Allen Tate and John Peale
    Bishop, eds. New York: L.B. Fischer, 1942.
    Contains: "Scyros."

D4 *New Poems, 1942.* Oscar Williams, ed. Mt. Vernon,
    New York: Peter Pauper Press, 1942. *Contains:*
    "Scyros," "The Fly," "Auto Wreck," "Buick," Mid-
    night Show."

D5 *American Decade.* Tom Boggs, ed. Cummington,
    Mass.: Cummington Press, 1943. *Contains:* "Term-
    inal," "Haircut," "Poet," "Satire: Anxiety."

D6 *New Poems, 1943.* Oscar Williams, ed. New York:
    Howell, Soskin, 1943. *Contains:* "The Dome of
    Sunday," "Elegy for Two Banjos," "University,"
    "Ballade of the Second-Best Bed," "Nostalgia."

D7 *Twentieth-Century American Poetry.* Conrad Aiken,
    ed. New York: Modern Library, 1944. *Contains:*
    "Nostalgia," "The Fly," "Epitaph for John and
    Richard," "Travelogue for Exiles," "The Twins,"
    "Poet," "Waitress."

D8 *A Comprehensive Anthology of American Poetry.*
    Conrad Aiken, ed. New York: Modern Library,
    1944. *Contains:* "Poet," "The Twins," "Travelogue
    for Exiles," "Nostalgia."

D9 *An Anthology of Famous English and American
    Poetry.* William Rose Benet and Conrad Aiken,
    eds. New York: Random House, 1944. *Contains:*
    "Poet," "The Twins," "Nostalgia," "Travelogue
    for Exiles."

D10 *The Zephyr Book of American Verse*. Ebba Dalin, ed. Stockholm: Continental Book Company, 1944. *Contains:* "Scyros," "Midnight Show."

D11 *The Best Poems of 1943*. Thomas Moult, ed. New York: Harcourt, Brace and Company, 1944. *Contains:* "New Guinea."

D12 *American Writing, 1943*. Alan Swallow, ed. Boston: Bruse Humphries, 1944. *Contains:* "Newsboy," "Nostalgia."

D13 *American Writing, 1944*. Helen F. Caukin and Alan Swallow, eds. Boston: Bruse Humphries, 1945. *Contains:* "The Leg," "Red Indian."

D14 *The Music Makers*. Stanton A. Coblentz, compiler. New York: Ackerman, 1945. *Contains:* "On Reading Keats in War Time."

D15 *War and the Poet*. Richard Eberhart and Selden Rodman, eds. New York: Devin-Adair Company, 1945. *Contains:* "Nostalgia," "Troop Train," "Elegy for a Dead Soldier."

D16 *Poet to Poet: A Treasury of Golden Criticism*. Houston Peterson and William S. Lynch, eds. Englewood Cliffs, N.J.: Prentice-Hall, Inc., 1945. *Contains:* "On Reading Keats in War Time," "Israfel."

D17 *Poet's Gold*. David Ross, ed. New York: Dial Press, 1945. *Contains:* "Travelogue for Exiles."

D18 *The War Poets: An Anthology of the War Poetry of the 20th Century*. Oscar Williams, ed. New York: The John Day Company, 1945. *Contains:* "Scyros," "V-Letter," "Troop Train," "Elegy for a Dead Soldier," "Elegy for Two Banjos," "The Dome of Sunday," "Introduction to *V-Letter and Other Poems.*"

D19 *A New Anthology of Modern Poetry*. Selden Rodman,

ed. New York: The Modern Library, 1946. *Contains:* from *Essay on Rime* [lines 1385-1401], "Auto Wreck," "The Fly," "Nigger," "The Leg," from *Essay on Rime* ["Form," "Speech and Poetry," "The Ratio of Rime to Language," "Belief and Poetry," "The Poetry of Ideas"].

D20   *A Little Treasury of Modern Poetry: English and American.* Oscar Williams, ed. New York: Charles Scribner's Sons, 1946. *Contains:* "Scyros," "Nostalgia," "Auto Wreck," "The Dome of Sunday," "The Fly."

D21   *Literature for Our Time.* Leonard S. Brown, Harlow O. Waite and Benjamin P. Atkinson, eds. New York: Henry Holt and Company, 1947. *Contains:* "Buick," "New Guinea Letter," "Elegy for a Dead Soldier."

D22   *Spearhead.* James Laughlin, ed. New York: New Directions, 1947. *Contains:* "Haircut," "Fireworks," "The Leg," "Poet's Chorus."

D23   *Better Reading 2: Literature.* Walter Blair and John C. Gerber, eds. Chicago: Scott, Foresman and Company, 1948. *Contains:* "Auto Wreck."

D24   *Readings for Liberal Education.* Louis G. Locke, William M. Gibson, and George Arms, eds. New York: Rinehart and Company, 1948. *Contains:* "University."

D25   *100 American Poems.* Selden Rodman, ed. New York: The New American Library, 1948. *Contains:* "Elegy for a Dead Soldier."

D26   *College Reader.* Homer A. Watt and Oscar Cargill, eds. New York: Peter Pauper Press, 1948. *Contains:* from *Essay on Rime* ["General and Personal Idiom"].

D27   *A Little Treasury of American Poetry.* Oscar Williams, ed. New York: Charles Scribner's Sons,

1948. *Contains:* "Scyros," "University," "Elegy
for Two Banjos."

D28 *This Generation.* George K. Anderson and Eda Lou
Waton, eds. Chicago: Scott, Foresman and Company,
1949. *Contains:* "Necropolis," "University," "The
"Twins," "V-Letter," "The Intellectual," "Jew,"
"Troop Train."

D29 *Dominant Types in British and American Literature.*
William H. Davenport, Lowry C. Wimberly, and
Harry Shaw, eds. New York: Harper & Brothers,
1949. *Contains:* "Buick," "Hollywood," "Contraband."

D30 *American Literature: An Anthology and Critical
Study.* Joe Lee Davis, John T. Frederick, and
Frank Luther Mott, eds. New York: Charles Scrib-
ner's Sons, 1949. *Contains:* "Troop Train," "The
Gun," "Sunday: New Guinea," from *Essay on Rime*
["The Confusion in Belief"].

D31 *The Critical Reader.* Wallace Douglas, Roy Lam-
son, and Hallett Smith, eds. New York: W.W.
Norton, 1949. *Contains:* "Boy-Man."

D32 *The Poetry of the Negro.* Langston Hughes and
Arna Bontemps, eds. Garden City, N.Y.: Double-
day, 1949. *Contains:* "Recapitulations," "The
Southerner."

D33 *100 Modern Poems.* Selden Rodman, ed. New York:
Pellegrini and Cudahy, 1949. *Contains:* "The
Progress of Faust."

D34 *The Spell of the Pacific.* Carl Stroven and A.
Grove Day, eds. New York: The Macmillan Company,
1949. *Contains:* "New Guinea."

D35 *Understanding Poetry.* Cleanth Brooks and Robert
Penn Warren. New York: Henry Holt and Company,
1950. *Contains:* "The Leg," "Case History of
'The Minute,'" "The Minute."

D36   *Mid-Century American Poets*. John Ciardi, ed.
New York: Twayne, 1950. *Contains:* "The Case
History of 'The Minute,'" "The Minute," "Home-
coming," "Elegy for a Dead Soldier," "V-Letter,"
"The Dirty Word," "Buick," "The Twins," "Full
Moon: New Guinea," "Washington Cathedral," "Auto
Wreck," "The Fly."

D37   *The Oxford Book of American Verse*. F.O. Matthies-
sen, ed. New York: Oxford University Press, 1950.
Contains: "The Dome of Sunday," "University,"
"Midnight Show," "Hollywood," "Drug Store,"
"Troop Train," "Nigger," "The Geographers,"
"Elegy for a Dead Soldier," "The Conscientious
Objector."

D38   *Reading Poetry*. Fred B. Millett. New York:
Harper & Brothers, 1950. *Contains:* "Poet."

D39   *Sound and Sense*. Laurence Perrine, ed. New
York: Harcourt, Brace and Company, 1950. *Contains:* "Boy-Man."

D40   *Modern American Poetry*. Louis Untermeyer, ed.
New York: Harcourt, Brace and Company, 1950.
Contains: "The Leg," "The Puritan," "Travelogue
for Exiles," "The Twins," "The Dome of Sunday,"
"October 1," "Poet." Note: A "Combined Edition"
with *Modern British Poetry* was published in 1942;
includes the same poems on the same pages.

D41   *The New Modern American & British Poetry*. Louis
Untermeyer, ed. New York: Harcourt, Brace and
Company, 1950. *Contains:* "Travelogue for Exiles,"
"The Leg."

D42   *A Little Treasury of Modern Poetry: English &
American*. Oscar Williams, ed. New York: Charles
Scribner's Sons, 1950. *Contains:* "Auto Wreck,"
"The Dome of Sunday," "Nostalgia," "Scyros,"
"The Fly."

D43   *Modern Poetry, American and British*. Kimon Friar

and John Malcolm Brinnin, eds. New York: Apple-
ton-Century-Crofts, Inc., 1951. *Contains:* "Elegy
Written on a Frontporch," "Haircut," "The Dome of
Sunday."

D44 *Writing from Observation.* George A. Peck, ed.
New York: Harcourt, Brace and Company, 1951.
Contains: "Auto Wreck."

D45 *British Literature.* Hazelton Spencer, Walter
Houghton, and Herbert Barrows, eds. Lexington,
Mass.: D.C. Heath and Company, 1952. *Contains:*
"The ABC of Prosody."

D46 *Poetry as Experience.* Norman C. Stageberg and
Wallace L. Anderson, eds. New York: American
Book Company, 1952. *Contains:* "Auto Wreck."

D47 *Immortal Poems of the English Language.* Oscar
Williams, ed. New York: The Pocket Library,
1952. *Contains:* "Scyros."

D48 *Approaches to Poetry.* Walter Blair and W.K.
Chandler, eds. New York: Appleton-Century-
Crofts, Inc., 1953. *Contains:* "The Minute."

D49 *Literature for Our Time.* Harlow O. Waite and
Benjamin P. Atkinson, eds. New York: Henry Holt
and Company, 1953. *Contains:* "Travelogue for
Exiles," "Elegy for a Dead Soldier," "Buick."

D50 *Reader and Writer.* Harrison Hayford and Howard
P. Vincent, eds. Boston: Houghton Mifflin Company, 1954. *Contains:* "University."

D51 *American Issues: Volume Two, The Literary Record.*
Willard Thorp, Merle Curti, and Carlos Baker, eds.
Chicago: J.B. Lippincott Company, 1954. *Contains:*
"My Grandmother," "Drug Store," "Poet," "Troop
Train."

D52 *The Pocket Book of Modern Verse.* Oscar Williams,
ed. New York: Pocket Books, 1954. *Contains:*

"Troop Train," "The Minute," "The Twins."

D53 *The College Anthology.* Walter Blair and John C.
Gerber, eds. Chicago: Scott, Foresman and Company, 1955. *Contains:* "Auto Wreck."

D54 *The Types of Literature.* Francis Connolly. New
York: Harcourt, Brace and Company, 1955. *Contains:* "Hollywood."

D55 *Reading Modern Poetry.* Paul Engle and Warren
Carrier, eds. Chicago: Scott, Foresman and
Company, 1955. *Contains:* "Christmas Eve," "Auto
Wreck," "Adam and Eve" ["The Sickness of Adam,"
"The Recognition of Eve," "The Kiss," "The Tree
of Guilt," "The Confession," "Shame," "Exile"].

D56 *The American Treasury 1954-1955.* Clifton Fadiman,
ed. New York: Harper & Brothers, 1955. *Contains:*
Excerpts from a letter from an army camp, from
"Elegy for a Dead Soldier," "University," "The
Conscientious Objector."

D57 *Selection: A Reader for College Writing.* Walter
Havighurst, Robert F. Almy, Gordon D. Wilson, and
L. Ruth Middlebrook, eds. New York: The Dryden
Press, Inc., 1955. *Contains:* "Troop Train," "The
Gun."

D58 *Interpreting Literature.* K.L. Knickerbocker and
H. Willard Reninger, eds. New York: Henry Holt
and Company, 1955. *Contains:* "University."

D59 *A Treasury of Great Poems: English and American.*
Louis Untermeyer, ed. New York: Simon and Schus-
ter, 1955. *Contains:* "The Leg," "Buick."

D60 *The New Pocket Anthology of American Verse: From
Colonial Days to the Present.* Oscar Williams,
ed. New York: The Pocket Library, 1955. *Contains:* "Auto Wreck," "The Dome of Sunday," "Scyros," "The Fly."

D61   *Theme and Form: An Introduction to Literature.*
Monroe Beardsley, Robert Daniel, and Glenn Leg-
gett, eds. Englewood Cliffs, N.J.: Prentice-
Hall, Inc., 1956. *Contains:* "The Leg."

D62   *The Growth of American Literature: A Critical
and Historical Survey.* Edwin Harrison Cady,
Frederick J. Hoffman, and Roy Harvey Pearce, eds.
New York: American Book Company, 1956. *Contains:*
"University," "Drug Store," "Troop Train."

D63   *Fifteen Modern American Poets.* George P. Elliot,
ed. New York: Rinehart & Company, Inc., 1956.
Contains: from "Adam and Eve," "Drug Store,"
"Haircut," "Love for a Hand," "Mongolian Idiot,"
"October 1," "The Southerner," "V-Letter," "Wait-
ress," "The Tingling Back," "Recapitulations."

D64   *Adventures in Modern Literature.* Robert Frier,
Arnold Leslie Lazarus, and Herbert Potell, eds.
New York: Harcourt, Brace and Company, 1956.
Contains: "Travelogue for Exiles," "Interlude
III."

D65   *A Quarto of Modern Literature.* Leonard Brown
and Porter G. Perrin, eds. New York: Charles
Scribner's Sons, 1957. *Contains:* "Adam and Eve"
["The Sickness of Adam," "The Recognition of Eve,"
"The Kiss," "The Tree of Guilt," "The Confession,"
"Shame," "Exile"].

D66   *American Poetry and Prose.* Norman Forester, ed.
Boston: Houghton Mifflin Company, 1957. *Contains:*
"University," "Hollywood," "Drug Store," "Elegy
for a Dead Soldier," "The Conscientious Objector."

D67   *Introduction to Literature: Readings for a Liberal Education.* Louis G. Locke, William M. Gibson,
and George Arms, eds. New York: Rinehart and
Company, 1957. *Contains:* "University," "Auto
Wreck," "Recapitulations."

D68   *Seven Centuries of Verse, English & American.*

A.J.M. Smith, ed. New York: Charles Scribner's Sons, 1957. *Contains:* "Scyros."

D69 *Modern Verse in English 1900-1950.* David Cecil and Allen Tate, eds. New York: The Macmillan Company, 1958. *Contains:* "Drug Store," "The Interlude," "The Fly," "Scyros," "Haircut," "Auto Wreck."

D70 *A College Book of Modern Verse.* James K. Robinson and Walter B. Rideout, eds. New York: Harper & Row, 1958. *Contains:* "The Dome of Sunday," "The Potomac," "Nostalgia," "Elegy for a Dead Soldier," "V-Letter," "The Sickness of Adam."

D71 *The Atlantic Book of British and American Poetry.* Dame Edith Sitwell, ed. Boston: Little, Brown and Company, 1958. *Contains:* "Elegy for Two Banjos."

D72 *The Pocket Book of Modern Verse.* Oscar Williams, ed. New York: Pocket Books, Inc., 1958. *Contains:* "The Minute."

D73 *Better Reading 2: Literature.* Walter Blair and John C. Gerber, eds. Chicago: Scott, Foresman and Company, 1959. *Contains:* "Auto Wreck."

D74 *Writing from Observation.* Lester Cameron and Samuel A. Golden, eds. New York: Harcourt, Brace and Company, 1959. *Contains:* "Auto Wreck," "The Twins."

D75 *How Does a Poem Mean?* John Ciardi, ed. Boston: Houghton Mifflin Company, 1959. *Contains:* "Scyros," "Buick."

D76 *Reader and Writer.* Harrison Hayford and Howard P. Vincent, eds. Boston: Houghton Mifflin Company, 1959. *Contains:* "University."

D77 *A Range of Writing.* Henry W. Knepler and Samuel K. Workman, eds. Englewood Cliffs, N.J.: Prentice-Hall, Inc., 1959. *Contains:* "Auto Wreck."

D78 *The Poem: A Critical Anthology.* Josephine Miles, ed. Englewood Cliffs, N.J.: Prentice-Hall, Inc., 1959. *Contains:* "The Twins."

D79 *A D.H. Lawrence Miscellany.* Harry T. Moore, ed. Carbondale: Southern Illinois University Press, 1959. *Contains:* "The Unemployed Magician."

D80 *Literature: An Introduction.* Hollis Summers and Edgar Whan, eds. New York: McGraw-Hill Book Company, Inc., 1960. *Contains:* "Buick," "Haircut," "The Alphabet."

D81 *Understanding Poetry.* Cleanth Brooks and Robert Penn Warren, eds. New York: Holt, Rinehart and Winston, Inc., 1960. *Contains:* "The Leg," "The Minute."

D82 *Poetry, Its Power and Wisdom: An Introductory Study.* Francis Connolly, ed. New York: Charles Scribner's Sons, 1960. *Contains:* "Buick."

D83 *Freshman English Program.* Cary B. Graham, ed. Chicago: Scott, Foresman and Company, 1960. *Contains:* "Auto Wreck."

D84 *Interpreting Literature.* K.L. Knickerbocker and H. Willard Reninger, eds. New York: Henry Holt and Company, 1960. *Contains:* "University."

D85 *Literary Themes and Types.* Maurice B. McNamee, James E. Cronin, and Joseph A. Rogers. New York: Rinehart & Company, 1960. *Contains:* "The Leg," "Hollywood."

D86 *Poetry for Pleasure: The Hallmark Book of Poetry.* Garden City, N.Y.: Doubleday & Company, 1960. *Contains:* "Auto Wreck," "Sunday: New Guinea."

D87 *A Casebook On Dylan Thomas.* John Malcolm Brinnin, ed. New York: Thomas Y. Crowell Company, 1960. *Contains:* "Dylan Thomas."

D88   *Famous Poems and the Little-Known Stories Behind
       Them.* Ralph L. Woods, ed. New York: Hawthorn
       Books, 1961. *Contains:* "Elegy for a Dead Soldier."

D89   *Modern Love Poems.* D.J. Klemer, ed. Garden City,
       N.Y.: Doubleday & Company, 1961. *Contains:* "The
       New Ring," "Love for a Hand," "V-Letter," "The
       Voyage."

D90   *E.E. Cummings and the Critics.* Stanley Baum, ed.
       Michigan: Michigan State University Press, 1962.
       Contains: "Prosody as the Meaning."

D91   *A Poetry Sampler.* Donald Hall, ed. New York:
       Franklin Watts, 1962. *Contains:* "The Twins."

D92   *Chief Modern Poets of England and America.* Gerald
       D. Sanders, John H. Nelson, M.L. Rosenthal, eds.
       New York: The Macmillan Company, 1962. *Contains:*
       "Drug Store," "The Dome of Sunday," "Auto Wreck,"
       "Buick," "Poet," "The Phenomenon," "Nostalgia,"
       "The Intellectual," "I sing the simplest flower."

D93   *The Dimensions of Poetry: A Critical Anthology.*
       James E. Miller, Jr. and Bernice Slote, eds.
       New York: Dodd, Mead & Company, 1962. *Contains:*
       "The Progress of Faust."

D94   *Poet's Choice.* Paul Engle and Joseph Langland,
       eds. New York: Dial Press, 1962. *Contains:*
       "The Dirty Word."

D95   *Erotic Poetry: The Lyrics, Ballads, Idylls, and
       Epics of Love, Classical to Contemporary.* William
       Cole, ed. New York: Random House, 1963. *Contains:* "The Confirmation."

D96   *Introduction to Literature: Poems.* Lynn Alten-
       bernd and Leslie L. Lewis, eds. New York: The
       Macmillan Company, 1963. *Contains:* "Drug Store,"
       "Auto Wreck," "Scyros."

D97   *The Penguin Book of Sick Verse.* George Macbeth,
       ed. New York: Penguin Books, 1963. *Contains:*

"The Fly."

D98   *American Lyric Poems: From Colonial Times to the
      Present.* Elder Olson, ed. New York: Appleton-
      Century-Crofts, 1964. *Contains:* "Auto Wreck,"
      "Terminal."

D99   *National Poetry Festival Held in the Library of
      Congress, October 22-24, 1962.* Reference Divi-
      sion, Library of Congress, ed. Washington, D.C.:
      Library of Congress, 1964. *Contains:* selections
      from *The Bourgeois Poet.*

D100 *The Contemporary Poet as Artist and Critic.*
      Anthony Ostroff, ed. Boston: Little, Brown and
      Company, 1964. *Contains:* "W.H. Auden's 'A Change
      of Air,'" notes on essays regarding *The Bourgeois
      Poet.*

D101 *Modern Religious Poems: A Contemporary Anthology.*
      Jacob Trapp, ed. New York: Harper & Row, 1964.
      Contains: "The Alphabet."

D102 *Today's Poets: American and British Poetry Since
      the 1930's.* Chad Walsh, ed. New York: Charles
      Scribner's Sons, 1964. *Contains:* "Elegy for a
      Dead Soldier," "August Saturday Night on the
      Negro Street," "The Recognition of Eve," "The
      Potomac," "Poet," "Love for a Hand," "Jew."

D103 *The Little Magazine and Contemporary Literature:
      A Symposium.* Reference Department, Library of
      Congress, ed. New York: Modern Language Associa-
      tion, 1965. *Contains:* "The Campus Literary Or-
      gan."

D104 *American Poetry.* Gay Wilson Allen, Walter B.
      Rideout, and James K. Robinson, eds. New York:
      Harper & Row, 1965. *Contains:* "Elegy for a Dead
      Soldier," "The Dome of Sunday," "The Sickness of
      Adam," "The Potomac," "Nostalgia," "V-Letter."

D105 *The Case for Poetry: A Critical Anthology.* Frederick L. Gwynn, Ralph W. Condee, and Arthur O. Lewis, eds. Englewood Cliffs, N.J.: Prentice-Hall, 1965. *Contains:* "As You Say," "Buick."

D106 *The Golden Journey: Poems for Young People.* Louise Bogan and William Jay Smith, eds. New York: Reilly and Lee, 1965. *Contains:* "Manhole Covers."

D107 *New Directions in Literature: A Study of Poetry.* Don M. Wolfe, ed. New York: McCormick-Mathers, 1965. *Contains:* "Buick."

D108 *New Directions in Literature: Introduction to Poetry.* Edgar H. Knapp, ed. New York: McCormick-Mathers, 1965. *Contains:* "Auto Wreck."

D109 *Poems and Poets.* David Aloian, ed. New York: McGraw-Hill, 1965. *Contains:* "Auto Wreck," "Full Moon: New Guinea."

D110 *Poems on Poetry.* Robert Wallace and James G. Taaffe, eds. New York: E.P. Dutton and Company, 1965. *Contains:* selection from *The Bourgeois Poet.*

D111 *The Earth Is the Lord's: Poems of the Spirit.* Helen Plotz, ed. New York: Thomas Y. Crowell Company, 1965. *Contains:* "The 151st Psalm," "The Murder of Moses."

D112 *This Land Is Mine: An Anthology of American Verse.* Al Hine, ed. New York: J.B. Lippincott Company, 1965. *Contains:* selection from "Elegy for a Dead Soldier," "V-Letter."

D113 *Dylan Thomas.* C.B. Cox, ed. Englewood Cliffs, N.J.: Prentice-Hall, 1966. *Contains:* "Dylan Thomas."

D114 *William Carlos Williams.* J.H. Miller, ed. Englewood Cliffs, N.J.: Prentice-Hall, 1966. *Contains:* "Study of 'Philomena Andronico.'"

D115   *Poetry in the Classroom.* Dorothy Petitt, ed. NP: National Council of Teachers of English, 1966. *Contains:* "Auto Wreck."

D116   *Voices of Protest and Hope.* Elisabeth D. Dodds, ed. NP: Friendship Press, 1966. *Contains:* "Elegy for a Dead Soldier."

D117   *The American Judaism Reader.* P. Kresh, ed. New York: Abelard-Schuman/Ram's Horn Books, 1967. *Contains:* "The Jewish Writer in America."

D118   *Randall Jarrell, 1914-1965.* Robert Lowell, Peter Taylor, and Robert Penn Warren, eds. New York: Farrar, Straus, and Giroux, Inc., 1967. *Contains:* "The Death of Randall Jarrell."

D119   *The New Modern Poetry.* M.L. Rosenthal, ed. New York: The Macmillan Company, 1967. *Contains:* "The Phenomenon."

D120   *Reflections on a gift of watermelon pickle and other modern verse.* Stephen Dunning, Edward Lueders, and Hugh Smith, eds. New York: Scholastic Book Services, 1967. *Contains:* "Interlude 3."

D121   *Heartland: Poets of the Midwest.* Lucien Stryk, ed. De Kalb, Ill.: Northern Illinois University Press, 1967. *Contains:* selections from *The Bourgeois Poet.*

D122   *America Forever New.* Sara Brewton and John E. Brewton, eds. New York: Thomas Y. Crowell, 1968. *Contains:* selection from "California Winter," "Americans are afraid of lizards," "Manhole Covers," "Sunday: New Guinea."

D123   *Cavalcade of Poems.* George Bennett and Paul Molloy, eds. New York: Scholastic Book Services, 1968. *Contains:* "Manhole Covers."

D124   *The Poem: An Anthology.* Stanley B. Greenfield and Kingsley Weatherhead, eds. New York: Appleton-Century-Crofts, 1968. *Contains:* "Christmas Eve: Australia," "Auto Wreck."

D125 *Poetry: An Introduction.* William G. Lane, ed. Lexington, Mass.: D.C. Heath, 1968. *Contains:* "There is a general idiom to all rime," "Wordsworth Imprisoned: on 'Nuns Fret Not,'" "An ABC of Prosody."

D126 *A Book of Nature Poems.* William Cole, ed. New York: The Viking Press, 1969. *Contains:* "A Cut Flower."

D127 *The Contemporary American Poets: American Poetry Since 1940.* Mark Strand, ed. New York: World Publishing Company, 1969. *Contains:* "The Dome of Sunday," "The Dirty Word," "Nostalgia," "Love for a Hand."

D128 *A Flock of Words.* David Mackay, ed. New York: Harcourt, Brace & World, 1969. *Contains:* "Auto Wreck."

D129 *A Gathering of Poems.* Maxwell Nurnberg, ed. New York: Washington Square Press, 1969. *Contains:* "Interlude iii."

D130 *Hold Fast to Dreams: Poems Old and New.* Arna Bontemps, ed. New York: Follett Publishers, 1969. *Contains:* "Manhole Covers."

D131 *The New Yorker Book of Poems.* New York: The Viking Press, 1969. *Contains:* "D.C.," "Christmas Eve: Australia," "Boy-Man," "The Bed," "The Progress of Faust," "The Poets of Hell," "The Phenomenon," "Love Letter" ["V-Letter"], "Love for a Hand," "In India," "The Southerner," "Western Town."

D132 *To Play Man Number One.* Sara Hannum and John Terry Chase, eds. New York: Atheneum, 1969. *Contains:* "The Leg."

D133 *Beach Glass and Other Poems.* Paul Molloy, ed.

NP: Four Winds Press, 1969. *Contains:* "Auto Wreck."

D134 *A Treasury of Yiddish Poetry.* Irving Howe and Eliezer Greenberg, eds. New York: Holt, Rinehart and Winston, 1969. *Contains:* 3 poems by Berish Weinstein ["Hunger," "Second Son," and "Sailors"] translated by K.S.

D135 *Sense and Sensibility in Twentieth-Century Writing.* Brom Weber, ed. Carbondale, Ill.: Southern Illinois University Press, 1970. *Contains:* "Cockfight in Milo" from *Edsel.*

D136 *A College Book of Verse.* C.F. Main, ed. New York: Wadsworth Publishing Company, 1970. *Contains:* "The Glutton," "The Twins."

D137 *A Little Treasury of Modern Poetry, English and American.* Oscar Williams, ed. New York: Charles Scribner's Sons, 1970. *Contains:* "The Dome of Sunday," "Auto Wreck," "The Fly," "Poet," "Hollywood," "Scyros," "Elegy for a Dead Soldier."

D138 *Men and Women: The Poetry of Love.* Louis Untermeyer, ed. New York: American Heritage Press, 1970. *Contains:* "Here ends this cycle of my poems for you."

D139 *Poetry in English.* Warren Taylor and Donald Hall, eds. New York: The Macmillan Company, 1970. *Contains:* "Glass Poem," "A Garden in Chicago," "Buick."

D140 *The Poetry of the Negro, 1746-1970.* Langston Hughes and Arna Bontemps, eds. Garden City, N.Y.: Doubleday and Company, 1970. *Contains:* "We waged a war within a war," "The Southerner."

D141 *Perspectives on Man: Kaleidoscope.* M. Jerry Weiss, ed. New York: Cummings Publication Company, 1970. *Contains:* "How do I love you?" "University."

D142 *Seven Centuries of Verse, English and American.*
A.J.M. Smith, ed. New York: Charles Scribner's
Sons, 1970. *Contains:* "Scyros."

D143 *Sounds and Silences: Poetry for Now.* Richard
Peck, ed. New York: Delacorte Press, 1970. *Contains:* "Auto Wreck," "The Conscientious Objector."

D144 *This Is My Best in the Third Quarter of the
Century.* Whit Burnett, ed. Garden City, N.Y.:
Doubleday and Company, 1970. *Contains:* "Adam
and Eve."

D145 *Twentieth Century Poetry: American and British
(1900-1970).* John Malcolm Brinnin and Bill Read,
eds. New York: McGraw-Hill Book Company, 1970.
Contains: "Drug Store," "Nostalgia," "Haircut."

D146 *Voices of Poetry.* Allen Kirschner, ed. New
York: Dell Publishers, 1970. *Contains:* "Auto
Wreck."

D147 *The Voice That Is Great Within Us.* Hayden Car-
ruth, ed. New York: Bantam Books, 1970. *Con-
tains:* "Hospital," "Auto Wreck," "My Grandmother,"
"The Jew at Christmas Eve," "The First Time,"
"Quintana lay in the shallow grave of coral,"
"All tropic places smell of mold," "Aubade."

D148 *Modern American Poetry.* Guy Owen, ed. Deland,
Fla.: Everett/Edwards, 1972. *Contains:* "William
Carlos Williams."

D149 *Composition and Literary Form: An Anthology.*
Nicholas A. Salerno and Daniel J. Meyer, eds.
New York: Winthrop Publishers, 1972. *Contains:*
"Jew," "University."

D150 *Getting into Poetry.* Morris Sweetkind, ed. NP:
Holbrook Press, 1972. *Contains:* "Auto Wreck."

D151 *Fine Frenzy.* Robert Baylor and Brenda Stokes,
eds. New York: McGraw-Hill, 1972. *Contains:*
"Auto Wreck."

D152   *Enough of Dying! Voices for Peace.* Kay Boyle
       and Justine Van Gundy, eds. New York: Dell,
       1972. *Contains:* "Homecoming."

D153   *What's in a Poem.* John Rylander and Edith Ry-
       lander, eds. Encino, Calif.: Dickenson Publish-
       ers, 1972. *Contains:* "The Dirty Word," "Drug
       Store."

D154   *The Liberating Form: A Handbook-Anthology of
       English and American Poetry.* Bert C. Bach,
       William A. Sessins, and William Walling, eds.
       New York: Dodd, Mead & Company, 1972. *Contains:*
       "The Intellectual."

D155   *Themes in American Literature.* Charles Genthe
       and George Keithley, eds. Lexington, Mass.:
       D.C. Heath, 1972. *Contains:* "Nostalgia."

D156   *100 American Poems.* Selden Rodman, ed. New
       York: The New American Library, 1972. *Contains:*
       "Elegy for a Dead Soldier."

D157   *The Modern Age: Literature.* Leonard Lief and
       James F. Light, eds. New York: Holt, Rinehart
       and Winston, 1972. *Contains:* "Drug Store,"
       "Hollywood," "University."

D158   *The Norton Anthology of Modern Poetry.* Robert
       O'Clair and Richard Ellmann, eds. New York:
       W.W. Norton & Company, 1973. *Contains:* "The
       Dome of Sunday," "The Fly," "Poet," "V-Letter,"
       "The Alphabet," "Lower the standard: that's my
       motto."

D159   *Leaves of Grass* [Norton Critical Edition]. Scul-
       ley Bradley and Harold W. Blodgett, eds. New
       York: W.W. Norton, 1973. *Contains:* "The First
       White Aboriginal."

D160   *The Norton Introduction to Literature: Poetry.*
       J. Paul Hunter, ed. New York: W.W. Norton,
       1973. *Contains:* "Auto Wreck."

D161 *The American Tradition in Literature, Volume 2.*
Sculley Bradley, Richmond Croom Beatty, E. Hudson
Long, and George Perkins, eds. New York: W.W.
Norton, 1974. *Contains:* "Scyros," "Auto Wreck,"
"Aubade."

D162 *On Being Jewish: American Jewish Writers from
Cahan to Bellow.* Daniel Walden, ed. Greenwich,
Conn.: Fawcett Publications, Inc., 1974. *Con-
tains:* "The 151st Psalm," "The Leg," "The Jew."

D163 *Introduction to Poetry.* William C. Cavanaugh,
ed. Dubuque, Iowa: Wm. C. Brown Company, 1974.
Contains: "Auto Wreck."

D164 *American Literature: Tradition and Innovation.*
Harrison T. Meserole, Walter Sutton, and Brom
Weber, eds. Lexington, Mass.: D.C. Heath and
Company, 1974. [Corrected edition, volume 4].
Contains: "Drug Store," "University," "Elegy
for a Dead Soldier," "The Conscientious Objector."

D165 *Structure and Meaning.* Anthony Dube, John Karl
Franson, Russell E. Murphy, and James W. Parins,
eds. Boston: Houghton Mifflin Company, 1976.
Contains: "University," "Drug Store."

D166 *Writing in the Margin: From Annotation to Critical Essay.* Ronald Primeau, ed. New York:
David McKay Company, 1976. *Contains:* "To Abolish Children."

D167 *Washington and the Poet.* Francis Coleman Rosenberger, ed. Charlottesville: University Press of
Virginia, 1977. *Contains:* "Washington Cathedral."

E. MATERIAL BY KARL SHAPIRO
   IN TRANSLATION

E1   "New Guinea Letter," *Sur*, No. 113-114 (March-
      April, 1944), 112-119. Translated into Spanish
      by A. Bioy Casares and J.L. Borges.

E2   "The Tingling Back," *Botteghe Oscure*, II (1948),
      50-51. Translated into Italian by "A.G."

E3   "The Leg," "Troop Train," "Recapitulations XIV,"
      Das Lot, V (May, 1951), 41-43. Translated into
      German by Kurt Erich Meurer, with a biographical
      note.

E4   "V-Letter," *Libertinage*, V (March-April, 1952),
      136-138. Article on K.S. in Dutch by W.F. van
      Leeuwen, poem in English.

E5   *Poetry and Poetry Criticism* ["A Cut Flower," "The
      Contraband," "The Twins," "The Fly," "Poet," "Scy-
      ros," "Nostalgia," "Necropolis," "Travelogue for
      Exiles," excerpt from *Essay on Rime*, "What Is a
      Real Poem" from "What the Poet Knows," and "The
      Career of a Poem," "Conversation with Karl Shapiro,
      Salzburg, 9 January, 1952"]. Rikutaro Fukuda,
      translator and editor. Tokyo: Pipō Series, 37,
      Kokubunsha. Translated into Japanese. Transla-
      tor's appendix includes three notes on K.S.

E6   "The Alphabet," "Israel," *Bitzaron: The Hebrew
      Monthly of America*, XXXVIII (September, 1958),
      158-159. Translated into Hebrew by ʟeonard D.
      Friedland.

E7   "Troop Train," *Achievement in American Poetry,
      1900-1950*. Louise Bogan, ed. Tokyo: Hyoron Sha,
      1958. Translated into Japanese by Ichiro Nishi-
      zaki and Masao Nagata.

E8   "A Telescope for the Emperor," *Eibungaku Fukei*,
      I (Winter, 1958), 9-35. Translated into Japanese
      by Rikutaro Fukuda. This one-act play has been
      published only in this Japanese translation. Per-
      formed in English May 22, 23, 1958, by the Exper-
      imental Theatre of the University of Nebraska.

E9   "Travelogue for Exiles," "Poet," *CZAS NIEPOKOJU.*
      Pawel Mayewski, editor and translator. New York:
      Criterion Books, 1958. Poems in English and Pol-
      ish; Shapiro's introduction is in Polish only.

E10   "Scyros," "151st Psalm," *Galleria: Rassegna Bimes-
      trale,* VIII (September–December, 1958), 300–302.
      Translated into Italian by Alfredo Rizzardi.
      English in footnotes.

E11   "Recent American Poetry," *America,* No. 28 (n.d.,
      1959?), 8–11. Translated into Russian by members
      of U.S. State Department.

E12   "The Power of the Little Magazines," *America,* No.
      29 (n.d., 1959?), 9–11. Translated into Russian
      as E11.

E13   "Writers Teach Literary Creativity," *Ameryka,* No.
      15 (n.d., 1960?), 12–13, 56–57. Translated into
      Polish as E11.

E14   "The Power of the Little Magazines," *Ameryka,* No.
      19 (n.d., 1960?), 51–53. Translated into Polish
      as E11.

E15   "The Geographers," "The Minute," *Nowa Kultura,* XI
      (January 24, 1960), 3. Translated into Polish by
      Jaroslaw M. Rymkiewicz.

E16   "A Telescope for the Emperor," *Mita Bungaku,* L
      (February, 1960), 34–60. Translated into Japanese
      by Rikutaro Fukuda [see E8].

E17   "A Telescope for the Emperor," *Nihon Mirai-ha,* No.
      92 (March, 1960), 6–19. Translated into Japanese
      by Rikutaro Fukuda [see E8].

E18   "Is Contemporary Poetry Sick?" *Gendai-shi Kenkyu,*
      No. 115 (June, 1960), 20–21; No. 116 (July, 1960),
      21–24. Translated into Japanese by Rikutaro Fu-
      kuda.

E19 "The Second-Best Bed," "The Gun," "The Voyage."
     Trente-Cinq Jeunes Poetes Americains. Translated
     by Alain Bosquet. Paris: Gallimard, 1960. Trans-
     lated into French, with English originals on fac-
     ing pages.

E20 "Introduction to *A Season in Hell.*" *Une Saison
     en Enfer.* Translated by Nicholas Spania. Athens:
     1962. Translated into Greek.

E21 Selections from "The Bourgeois Poet," *Tematy*, No.
     7 (1963), 7-18. Translated into Polish by Waclaw
     Iwaniuk.

E22 "Drug Store," "Auto Wreck." *53 American Poets of
     Today.* Ruth Witt-Diamant and Rikutaro Fukuda, eds.
     Tokyo: Kenkyusha, 1968. Translated into Japanese.

E23 "Homecoming," "A Cut Flower." *Amerikanske Stemmer.*
     Jens Nyholm, ed. Sweden: Arne Frost-Hansens For-
     lag, 1968. Translated into Swedish.

E24 *In Defense of Ignorance* [*In Difesa Dell'Ignoranza*].
     Translated by Luigi Ballerini. Rome: Lerici
     editore, 1968.

APPENDIX
A Checklist of Selected Criticism & Reviews
of the Work of Karl Shapiro

compiled by David Huwiler

I. BIOGRAPHY AND CRITICISM

Aiken, Conrad. "Karl Shapiro." In *A Reviewer's ABC*, introduced by Rufus A. Blandshard. New York: Meridian Books, 1958, pp. 358-364. Aiken's essay deals with *Essay on Rime*, of which he says: "If one finds it sometimes *too* near the prose level, and certainly oftener pedestrian than equestrian, and if it far too seldom delights the ear, nevertheless it is very cunningly calculated for its purpose: and it is questionable whether, by tightening and formalizing it further, more might not have been lost than gained."

Angoff, Allan. *American Writing Today: Its Independence and Vigor*. New York: New York University Press, 1957, pp. 14, 21, 22, 71, 209, 210.

Bartlett, Phyllis. *Poems in Process*. New York: Oxford University Press, 1951, pp. 115-116, 139-140. Details the development of "The Fly" from its beginnings in Shapiro's notes.

Bloom, Edward A., Charles H. Philbrick II, and Elmer M. Blistein. *The Order of Poetry: An Introduction*. New York: Odyssey Press, 1961, pp. 23-28. The book contains an analysis of "Auto Wreck."

Bradley, Samuel M. "Letter to Karl Shapiro on Belief and Being." *Approach: A Literary Quarterly*, No. 33 (Fall, 1959), pp. 28-30.

Bradley, Samuel. "Shapiro Strikes at the Establishment." *UKCR*, XXIX (1963), pp. 275-279.

Cargas, Harry J. "Daniel Berrigan and the Ideas Found in Contemporary Anti-Establishment Poetry." *DAI* 32: 957A (St. Louis). Dissertation includes sections on Eberhart, Ginsberg, LeRoi Jones, Robert Lowell, and Karl Shapiro.

Coleman, Alice. "'Doors leap open.'" *EJ*, LIII (November, 1964), pp. 631-633. Coleman discusses the value of Shapiro's "Auto Wreck" as a pedagogical tool in a high school poetry class.

Daiches, David. "On Shapiro's 'Christmas Eve: Australia.'" In *Readings for Liberal Education*, ed. Louis G. Locke, William M. Gibson, and George Arms. New York: Rinehart and Company, 1952, pp. 270-271.

Daiches, David. "The Poetry of Karl Shapiro." *Poetry*,
LXVI (August, 1945), pp. 266-273. Critics, Daiches
says, tend to demand full-blown genius even from
young writers. "Shapiro is doing all right, working his passage to salvation the hard way. The
critics should take an interest in how he is doing
this and stop worrying about whether he is the finest young American poet."

Eckman, Frederick. "Karl Shapiro's 'Adam and Eve.'"
University of Texas Studies in English, XXXV (1956),
pp. 1-10.

Engle, Paul. "Five Years of Pulitzer Poets." *English
Journal*, XXXVIII (February, 1949), pp. 59-66. In
his one page on Shapiro, Engle emphasizes the "ex-
actitude" of Shapiro's poetry and the poet's con-
sistent reliance upon concrete things as opposed to
vague abstraction.

Fussell, Edwin. "Karl Shapiro: The Paradox of Prose
and Poetry." *Western Review*, XVIII (Spring, 1954),
pp. 225-244. A general discussion of Shapiro's pre-
1954 work with emphasis on Shapiro's conception of
the relationship between prose and poetry. Bibliography.

Glassberg, Rose. "Karl Shapiro: Poet Versus Critic."
DAI 33: 5722A-23A (Temple, 1972). Glassberg feels
that the best of Shapiro's poems accommodate the
two aspects of his personality: his desire to write
lyrical poetry and his inclination towards social
criticism. These poems reveal both Shapiro's "per-
sonalism" and his use of elements of formalistic
verse to "uncover the poetry of his immediate world."

Glicksberg, Charles I. "Karl Shapiro and the Personal
Accent." *Prairie Schooner*, XXII (Spring, 1948), pp.
44-52. Shapiro's "personal accent" is refreshing
in an age when "poetry has become deliberately anon-
ymous, eccentric, freakishly experimental, steeped
in the Surrealist juices of the unconscious."

Keltner, Jeanie E. "Karl Shapiro: The Bourgeois Poet."
DAI 34: 5179A (UCLA, 1973). Attempts to define
Shapiro as a poet caught between the two contra-
dictory tendencies which Stephen Spender has called
Modern and Contemporary.

Kohler, Dayton. "Karl Shapiro: Poet in Uniform."

College English, VII (February, 1946), 243-249.
"There are signs in *Essay on Rime* that Shapiro is
freeing himself from his apprenticeship in language
and form," and "Shapiro has the chance to become
the spokesman of his war generation."

Malkoff, Karl. "The Self in the Modern World: Karl
Shapiro's Jewish Poems." In *Contemporary American
Jewish Literature*. Bloomington: Indiana University
Press, 1973. For Shapiro, Malkoff argues, being a Jew
is the *consciousness* of being a Jew. "A metaphor
begins to emerge in which Jew comes to represent a
particular quality of mind, one that is intimately
related to the creative process. We are dealing
with an aspect of consciousness that is conscious
of itself, that is, in fact, obsessed with itself;
it is 'the primitive ego of the human race,' at-
tempting to survive against 'a background of nothing.'"

O'Connor, William Van. "Karl Shapiro: The Development
of a Talent." *College English*, X (November, 1948),
pp. 71-77. O'Connor traces the development of Shapiro's poetic tone from that of simple and unqual-
ified ironic detachment to that of sympathetic and
mature complexity and ambiguity.

O'Connor, William Van. "Shapiro's Southwest Pacific
Poem." *Poetry*, LXIV (September, 1944), pp. 326-334.
O'Connor praises Shapiro's happy delight in the
sensuous--"the body, its laughter and sins, its
parts and its coming to dust." He goes on the say
that "Shapiro is fortunate to follow upon the transi-
tion from sterile prudery through bald reaction, to
an easy acceptance of the human organism."

Pearce, Roy Harvey. *The Continuity of American Poetry*.
Princeton: Princeton University Press, 1961. Pearce
makes only brief mention of *Essay on Rime*, which he
calls a "manifesto posing as a meditation."

Reid, Alfred S. "The Southern Exposure of Karl Shapiro." *Southern Humanities Review*, VI (1972), pp.
35-44. Reid says that although we think of Shapiro
as a poet of urbanism, Jewishness, and bourgeois
banality, in the 1940s he wrote many poems which
reflect his exposure to Southern culture. After
1950, when Shapiro left the South, he gave up fur-

ther direct treatment of the region.

Rubin, Louis D., Jr. "The Search for Lost Innocence: Karl Shapiro's *The Bourgeois Poet.*" *Hollins Critic*, I, V, pp. 1-16. Rubin says that *TBP* is a failed attempt by Shapiro to use his critical discoveries to good advantage. In spite of Shapiro's mastery of the language, he fails to find an authentic, personal voice in *TBP*.

Scannell, Vernon. "The Poetry of Karl J. Shapiro." *Adelphi*, XXV (January-March, 1949), pp. 157-158.

Seif, Morton. "Poet's Journey: The Struggle in the Soul of Karl Shapiro." *Menorah Journal*, XXXVII (Winter, 1949), pp. 51-58.

Shafter, Toby. "Karl Shapiro, Poet in Khaki." *National Jewish Monthly* (April, 1948), pp. 288-291. Contains some biographical material.

Shockley, Martin. "Shapiro's Worlds." *American Literature*, XXI (January, 1950), p. 485. A note concerning the history of a misprint in "Nostalgia."

Slotkin, Richard. "The Contextual Symbol: Karl Shapiro's Image of 'The Jew.'" *American Quarterly*, XVIII, pp. 220-226. In *Poems of a Jew*, Slotkin argues, Shapiro tries to make the Jew a symbol for modern man. But, Slotkin continues, Shapiro alternates between the synagogue and the cathedral. Shapiro's perplexity "too often leads him to stridency in defense, or causes him to abandon the attempt to wring meaning out of large enigmas."

Smith, Hammett W. "Karl J. Shapiro: A Poet in Human Relations." *CLA Journal*, I (March, 1958), pp. 97-100.

Southworth, James G. "The Poetry of Karl Shapiro." *English Journal*, LI (March, 1962), pp. 159-166.

Stauffer, Donald Barlow. *A Short History of American Poetry.* New York: E.P. Dutton, 1974. Contains a brief history of Shapiro's career through *The Bourgeois Poet.*

Stepanchev, Stephen. *American Poetry Since 1945.* New York: Harper & Row, 1965. Contains a chapter on Shapiro. Stepanchev concludes that Shapiro's finest work belongs to the period 1940-1948.

Thornburg, Thomas R. "The Man with the Hatchet: Shapiro on Auden." *Ball State University Forum*, XI

(1970), pp. 25-34.

Van de Water, Charlotte. "A Soldier Poet." *Senior Scholastic*, XLVII (October 1, 1945), p. 19. An article written for high school students. Contains biographical material.

Vinavert, Michael. "Shapiro's 'Poet.'" *The Explicator*, IV (December, 1945), Item 23.

Waggoner, Hyatt H. *American Poets from the Puritans to the Present*. Boston: Houghton Mifflin, 1968. Waggoner includes a substantial section on Shapiro. He concludes that Shapiro has produced little during the past fifteen years because he has devoted so much energy to "denouncing his poetic fathers."

Williams, William Carlos. "Shapiro Is All Right." *Kenyon Review*, VIII (Winter, 1946), pp. 123-126. An impressionistic and reservedly appreciative discussion of *Essay on Rime*.

II. REVIEWS

The Place of Love

Crozier, Cecily. *A Comment*, No. 14 (January, 1943), p. 23.

Harris, Max. *A Comment*, No. 15 (March, 1943), pp. 22-23.

Person, Place and Thing

Bogan, Louise. *The New Yorker*, XVIII (January 9, 1943), pp. 45-46.

Christesen, Clement B. *Meanjin Papers*, II (Summer, 1943), p. 55.

Cowley, Malcolm. *Poetry*, LXI (February, 1943), pp. 620-622.

De Vries, Peter. *Chicago Sun Book Week*, I (December 6, 1942), p. 21.

Estes, Rice. *Library Journal*, LXVII (November 15, 1942), p. 1012.

Ghiselin, Brewster. *Accent*, III (Winter, 1943), p. 128.
Gregory, Horace. *Sewanee Review*, LII (Autumn, 1944),
    pp. 591-592.
Jack, Peter M. *The New York Times Book Review*, XLVIII
    (January 3, 1943), p. 11.
Lechlitner, Ruth. *New York Herald Tribune Books*, XIX
    (February, 1943), p. 18.
Mizener, Arthur. *Chimera*, II (Autumn, 1943), pp. 41-43.
Rodman, Selden. *The New Republic*, CVII (December 21,
    1942), p. 834.
Rosenberger, Francis Coleman. *Voices*, No. 113 (Spring,
    1943), pp. 56-60.
Schwartz, Delmore. *The Nation*, CLVI (January 9, 1943),
    pp. 63-64.
Tate, Allen. *Common Sense*, XII (February, 1943), pp.
    67-68.
Walton, Geoffrey. *Scrutiny*, XII (Autumn, 1944), pp.
    320-321.

V-Letter

Aiken, Conrad. *The New Republic*, CXI (October 23,
    1944), pp. 528-530.
Dupee, F.W. *The Nation*, CLIX (September 16, 1944), pp.
    327-328.
F., N. *Canadian Forum*, XXIV (December, 1944), pp. 213-
    214.
Flint, F. Cudworth. *The New York Times Book Review*,
    XLIX (September 3, 1944), pp. 4, 13.
Gregory, Horace. *Sewanee Review*, LII (Autumn, 1944),
    pp. 591-592.
Jones, Frank. *Briarcliff Quarterly*, I (January, 1945),
    pp. 233-234.
Kennedy, Leo. *Chicago Sun Book Week*, II (September,
    1944), p. 4.
Koch, Vivienne. *New York Herald Tribune Weekly Book
    Review*, XXI (October 29, 1944), p. 14.
Matthiessen, F.O. *Kenyon Review*, VI (Autumn, 1944),
    pp. 683-696.
Schwartz, Allen D. *Voices*, No. 120 (Winter, 1945),
    pp. 51-52.
Untermeyer, Louis. *Yale Review*, XXXIV (December, 1944),
    pp. 341-346.

Weiss, T. *Quarterly Review of Literature*, II (Summer, 1945), pp. 155-164.

Williams, Oscar. *Tomorrow*, IV (November, 1944), p. 86.

Baltimore Evening Sun (August 24, 1944), p. 30.

The New Yorker, XX (September 30, 1944), pp. 79-80.

Virginia Kirkus Bookshop Service, XII (July 1, 1944), p. 291.

Essay on Rime

Conrad Aiken. *The New Republic*, CXIII (December 3, 1945), pp. 752, 754.

Barrett, William. *Partisan Review*, XIII (Winter, 1946), pp. 126-129.

Daiches, David. *New York Herald Tribune Books*, XXII (January 6, 1946), p. 5.

Fitts, Dudley. *Poetry*, LXVIII (April, 1946), pp. 39-44.

Kennedy, Leo. *Chicago Sun Book Week*, II (November 4, 1945), p. 4.

Klein, A.M. *Northern Review*, I (October-November, 1946), pp. 30-38.

Matthiessen, F.O. *The New York Times Book Review*, L (October 28, 1945), p. 1.

Norse, Harold. *Tomorrow*, V (February, 1946), p. 74.

O'Connor, William Van. *Kenyon Review*, VIII (Winter, 1946), pp. 113-122.

Raskolenko, Harry. *Accent*, VI (1946), pp. 139-140.

Richman, Robert. *Sewanee Review*, LIV (October, 1946), pp. 684-690.

Schwartz, Delmore. *The Nation*, CLXI (November 10, 1945), p. 498.

Spencer, Theodore. *Saturday Review of Literature*, XXVIII (November 24, 1945), pp. 8-9, 34-35.

Stern, Peggy. *Commonweal*, XLIII (December 28, 1945), p. 292.

Untermeyer, Louis. *Yale Review*, XXXV (Winter, 1946), pp. 335-338.

Williams, William Carlos. *Kenyon Review*, VIII (Winter, 1946), 123-126.

Booklist, XLII (February 1, 1946), p. 181.

Christian Science Monitor (January 12, 1946), p. 17.

The New Yorker, XXI (December 29, 1945), p. 446.

Trial of a Poet

Adams, Walter Wood. *Voices*, No. 134 (Summer, 1948), pp. 52–54.

Arrowsmith, William. *Hudson Review*, I (Spring, 1948), pp. 98–105.

Bogan, Louise. *The New Yorker*, XXVIII (November 15, 1947), pp. 130–134.

Bunker, Robert. *New Mexico Quarterly Review*, XVIII (Spring, 1948), pp. 116–117.

Davidson, Eugene. *Yale Review*, XXXVII (June, 1948), pp. 745–750.

Fitzgerald, Robert. *The New Republic*, CXVIII (January 5, 1948), pp. 25–26.

Holden, Raymond. *Saturday Review of Literature*, XXXI (March 20, 1948), p. 16.

Jarrell, Randall. *The Nation*, CLXVII (July 17, 1948), pp. 80–81.

McDonald, Gerald. *Library Journal*, LXXII (December 1, 1947), p. 1688.

Rago, Henry. *Commonweal*, XLVII (January 16, 1948), pp. 352–354.

Rodman, Selden. *The New York Times Book Review*, LII (November 9, 1947), p. 6.

Spender, Stephen. *Poetry*, LXXI (March, 1948), pp. 314–318.

Bookshelf, XLIV (December 1, 1947), p. 131.

Christian Science Monitor (February 21, 1948), p. 15.

Cleveland Open Shelf (November, 1947), p. 21.

United States Quarterly Book List, IV (June, 1948), pp. 142–143.

Virginia Kirkus Bookshop Service, XV (August 15, 1947), p. 461.

A Bibliography of Modern Prosody

Ghiselin, Brewster. *Poetry*, LXXII (September, 1948), pp. 332–335.

Holden, Raymond. *Saturday Review of Literature*, XXXI (March 20, 1948), p. 16.

The Times Literary Supplement, No. 2, 451 (January 22, 1949), p. 62.

Poems 1940-1953

Bennett, Joseph. *Hudson Review*, VII (Summer, 1954),
   pp. 300-308.
Bogan, Louise. *The New Yorker*, XXX (June 5, 1954), pp.
   133-135.
Ciardi, John. *The Nation*, CLXXVII (November 14, 1953),
   p. 410.
Deutsch, Babette. *The New York Herald Tribune Book
   Review*, XXX (January 10, 1954), p. 12.
Deutsch, Babette. *Yale Review*, XLIII (December, 1953),
   pp. 276-281.
Engle, Paul. *Chicago Sunday Tribune* (October 4, 1953),
   p. 10.
Ferling, Lawrence. *San Francisco Chronicle* (November
   29, 1953), p. 20.
Fussell, Edwin. *Talisman*, No. 5 (Summer, 1954), pp.
   27-30.
McDonald, Gerald. *Library Journal*, LXXVIII (December
   15, 1953), p. 2221.
Redman, Ben Ray. *Saturday Review*, XXXVI (December 12,
   1953), p. 27.
Rodman, Selden. *The New York Times Book Review*, LVIII
   (October 11, 1953), p. 5.
Rosenberger, Francis Coleman. *Voices*, No. 154 (May-
   August, 1954), pp. 35-37.
Booklist, L (November 1, 1953), p. 96.
Bookmark, XIII (November, 1953), p. 34.

Beyond Criticism

Deutsch, Babette. *The New York Herald Tribune Book
   Review*, XXX (January 10, 1954), p. 12.
Engle, Paul. *Chicago Sunday Tribune* (November 15,
   1954), p. 6.
Geiger, Don. *Quarterly Journal of Speech*, XL (April,
   1954), pp. 210-211.
Mizener, Arthur. *Sewanee Review*, LXII (July, 1954),
   pp. 504-509.
Rodman, Selden. *The New York Times Book Review*, LVII
   (October 11, 1953), p. 5.
Rosenberger, Francis Coleman. *Voices*, No. 154 (May-

August, 1954), pp. 35-37.
Booklist, L (November, 1953), p. 95.

Poems of a Jew

Berryman, John. *American Scholar*, XXVIII (Summer, 1959), pp. 384-390).

Blocker, Joel. *Jerusalem Post* (March 6, 1959), np.

Ciardi, John. *Saturday Review*, XLI (September 27, 1958), pp. 17-19.

Deutsch, Babette. *The New York Herald Tribune Book Review*, XXXIV (July 20, 1958), p. 8.

Engle, Paul. *Chicago Sunday Tribune* (July 6, 1958), p. 3.

Feldman, Irving. *Commentary*, XXVI (November, 1958), pp. 447-448.

Fiedler, Leslie A. *Poetry*, XCVI (June, 1960), pp. 171-178.

Grieg, Michael. *San Francisco Examiner* (May 3, 1959), p. 43.

Gunn, Thom. *Yale Review*, XLVIII (December, 1958), pp. 297-305.

Lauter, Paul. *The New Republic*, CXXXIX (November 24, 1958), pp. 18-19.

Logan, John. *Commonweal*, LXVIII (September 19, 1958), pp. 620-621.

Maddocks, Melvin. *Christian Science Monitor* (July 24, 1958), p. 5.

McDonald, Gerald D. *Library Journal*, LXXXIII (June 15, 1958), p. 1938.

Rosenthal, M.L. *The Nation*, CLXXXVII (July 5, 1958), pp. 14-15.

Thompson, John. *Hudson Review*, XI (Autumn, 1958), pp. 443-450.

Wolf, Leonard. *The New York Times Book Review*, LXIII (September 7, 1958), p. 10.

Booklist, LIV (July 15, 1958), p. 633.

Virginia Kirkus Bookshop Service, XXVI (April 1, 1958), p. 307.

In Defense of Ignorance

Brown, Merle. *Christian Century*, LXXVII (September,
    1960), p. 1059.
Carruth, Hayden. *New Republic*, CXLII (June 20, 1960),
    p. 19.
Dorn, N.K. *San Francisco Chronicle* (July 10, 1960),
    p. 29.
Ellmann, Richard. *New York Times Review of Books* (May
    8, 1960), p. 10.
Langbaum, Robert. *The New York Herald Tribune Book
    Review* (May 8, 1960), p. 9.
Logan, John. *Commonweal*, LXXIII (January 20, 1960),
    p. 438.
Maddocks, Melvin. *Christian Science Monitor* (July 14,
    1960), p. 7.
Rosenthal, M.L. *The Nation*, CXCI (September 24, 1960),
    p. 184.
Wermuth, P.C. *Library Journal*, LXXXV (August, 1960),
    p. 2792.
Booklist, LVI (July 1, 1960), p. 650.
Kirkus, XXVIII (March 15, 1960), p. 254.

The Bourgeois Poet

Bogan, Louise. *New Yorker*, XL (November 7, 1964),
    p. 238.
Cutler, Bruce. *Prairie Schooner* (Winter, 1964), p.
    363.
Elliott, George P. *Hudson Review* (Autumn, 1964), p.
    462.
Friedberg, M. *Chicago Sunday Tribune* (June 7, 1964),
    p. 10.
Howard, Richard. *Poetry* (June, 1965), p. 225.
John, Godfrey. *Christian Science Monitor* (July 30,
    1964), p. 5.
McCauley, Robie. *New York Times Book Review* (November
    15, 1964), p. 71.
Scarbrough, George. *Sewanee Review* (Winter, 1965),
    p. 138.
Schott, Webster. *The Nation* (August 24, 1964), p. 74.
Smith, Ray. *Library Journal*, LXXXIX (June 1, 1964),
    p. 2352.
Smith, W.J. *Harper's*, CCXXIX (August, 1964), p. 99.

Stepanchev, Stephen. *Book Week* (August 2, 1964), p. 16.

To Abolish Children

Cevasco, G.A. *Library Journal*, XCIII (April 15, 1968), p. 1633.
Fussell, Paul. *Partisan Review* (Winter, 1969), p. 141.
Lieberman, L. *Poetry* (February 7, 1969), p. 346.
Obermyer, Janet. *Christian Science Monitor* (August 6, 1968), p. 9.
Sisk, J.P. *Commonweal*, LXXXIX (October 4, 1968), p. 32.
New York Times Book Review (August 18, 1968), p. 31.
Time, XCII (August 2, 1968), p. 66.

White-Haired Lover

Demos, John. *Library Journal*, XCIII (September 1, 1968), p. 3014.
Hoffman, Daniel. *Poetry*, CXIV (August, 1969), p. 336.
Justus, J.H. *Southern Review* (Winter, 1973), p. 261.
Ricks, C. *The Massachusetts Review* (Spring, 1970), p. 313.
Roskelenko, H. *Chicago Jewish Forum* (Winter, 1968-1969), p. 141.
Spector, R.D. *Saturday Review*, LII (March 15, 1969), p. 34.
Choice, VI (May, 1969), p. 370.
Time, XCIII (January 24, 1969), p. 72.
Virginia Quarterly Review, XLV (Winter, 1969), p. xvi.

Selected Poems

Carruth, Hayden. *New York Times Book Review* (July 14, 1968), p. 10.
Lieberman, L. *Poetry* (April, 1969), p. 44.
Mayo, E.L. *Northwest Review* (Fall, 1970), p. 114.
Mills, Ralph. *Modern Age* (Fall, 1968), p. 423.
Walsh, C. *Book World* (July 28, 1968), p. 4.

Edsel

Broyard, A. *New York Times Book Review* (October 4, 1971), p. 41.
Charles, J.W. *Library Journal*, XCVI (September 15, 1971), p. 2794.
Donoghue, D. *New York Review of Books* (December, 1971), p. 28.
Kinieri, Paul. *Best Sellers*, XXXI (October 1, 1971), p. 304.
Mano, D.K. *National Review*, XXIII (September 24, 1971), p. 1062.
Maloff, Saul. *New Republic*, CLXV (September 4, 1971), p. 30.
Moscoso-Gongora, Peter. *New York Times Book Review* (November 28, 1971), p. 53.
Reiss, James. *Saturday Review*, LIV (September 11, 1971), p. 44.
Antioch Review (Fall, 1971), p. 439.

The Poetry Wreck

Bedient, C. *Hudson Review* (Autumn, 1975), p. 459.
Broyard, A. *New York Times Review of Books* (March 13, 1975), p. 43.

Adult Bookstore

Cotter, J.F. *America*, CXXXV (November 20, 1976), p. 356.
Flint, R.W. *New York Times Review of Books* (July 25, 1976), p. 6.
Guereschi, Edward. *Best Sellers*, XXXVI (August, 1976), p. 167.
Madigan, Michael. *Library Journal*, CI (April 1, 1976), p. 904.
Choice, XIII (October, 1976), p. 828.
Virginia Quarterly Review, LII (Autumn, 1976), p. 118.

TITLE INDEX

Items are indexed by entry numbers. Titles of Shapiro's books, pamphlets, and broadsides (including those edited, co-authored, or introduced) are in italics. Material in anthologies and translations are not included.

"Flower, A" A2
"Fly, The" A3, A16
"Flying First Class" A23, C230
"Foot, The" B12
"Foot in the Door, A" C181
"Forethought, The" A1
"Foreword" [to *A Prosody Handbook*] B12
"Franklin" A4, A16
"Free Verse" B12
"French poetry that always goes itself one better" A13, A16
"From the Catechuman: A First Year Man's Philosophy" C1
"From the top floor of the Tulsa hotel" A13, A16, C164
"Fugue, And" A1
"Full Moon: New Guinea" A4, A9, A16, C37

"Garage Fool, The" A23, C231
"Garage Sale" A23, C218
"Garden in Chicago, A" A16, C160
"Genesis" A1
"Geographers, The" A4
"Giantess" A3, A9, A16, C21
"Girls Working in Banks" A23, C231
"Gladdith Anon Thou Lusty Troynovaunt" A1
"Glass Poem" A9, A16
"Glossary" [to *A Prosody Handbook*] B12
"Glottal as a bottle, everybody loves you"
A13, A16
"Glutton, The" A3, A9, A16
"God couldn't stand the sight of Cain" A13, A16
"Going to School" A16, C16, C101
"Good Friday Music" C214
"Greatest Living Author, The" A12
"Greatest Living Patagonian, The" A22, B7
"Guineapig" A16
"Gun, The" A4, A9, A16, C29

"Hair" C221
"Hair Stylist of a Generation" C216
"Haircut" A3, A9, A16, C19
"Ham-Bone of a Saint, The" A11
Harlem Gallery B13
"Hart Crane, though handicapped, did well" A13, A16
"He Loves the Chase" A19
"He-Man" C70
"He said it: Kill the poet in yourself" A13, A16
"Heiligenstadt Testament, The" A23, C236
"Henry Miller: Important Reprints" C170
"Hill at Parramatta" A4, A9, A16, C24, C26
"History of Philosophy professor is a fashion plate, The" A14, A16
"Hollywood" A3, A9, A16, B1, C211
"Homage to Calder" C108
"Homecoming" A7, A9, A16, C64
"Honeymoon" C61

Bohemian, The" C217
"Poet as Hero, The" C193
"Poet Dissects the Modern Poets, A" C65
"Poet takes the voyage to the New Cytherea, The" A13, A16
"Poetry and Verse" B12
"Poetry in 1956" C131
"Poetry of Bob Dylan" C237
"Poetry of Spilled Blood, The" C201
"Poetry Reading, The" A16, C118
Poetry Wreck, The A22
"Poetry Wreck, The" A22, C219
"Poets, Society, and Religion" C212
"Poets and Psychologists" A12, C109
Poets at Work B2
"Poet's Joy, The" C194
"Poets of Hell" C80
"Poets of the Cosmic Consciousness" A12
"Poets of the Silent Generation" C138
"Pop, Kid Stuff, & Poetry" C200
"Portrait of My Hand" A2, C36
"Posterity is a literary racket" A13, A16
"Potomac, The" A9, A16
"Preachers (say Episcopal), The" A13, A16
"Preface" [to *The Place of Love*] A2
"Pressed Flower" A2
"Priests and Freudians will understand"

A13, A16
Primer for Poets, A A10
"Progress Of Faust" A7, A9, A11, A16, B3, C77
"Property" A3, C2
"Prophets say to know Thyself, The" A13
Prose Keys to Modern Poetry B10
"Prosody and Period" B12
"Prosody as a Study" B12
"Prosody as the Meaning" C97
Prosody Handbook, A B12
"Prostitute" A1
"Proud of my half-education now" A13
"Psalm, The 151st" A11
"Public Library" A4, C44, C57
"Public Transit" A1
"Puritan, The" A4, C54, C56

"Question of the Pound Award, The" C99
"Quintana lay in the shallow grave of coral" A13, A16

"Race, The" C221
"Radical Rich, The" C221
"Randall, I like your poetry terribly" A13, A16
Randall Jarrell A14
"Rape of Philomel, The" A23
"Recapitulations" A7, A9, A16, C81
"Recognition of Eve, The" B3, C107
"Red Indian" A4, A9, A16, C41
"Reeking with Love" A19, C214

194